THEN AND THERE SERIES
GENERAL EDITOR
MARJORIE REEVES

Muhammad and the World of Islam

H O A McWILLIAM

Illustrated from contemporary sources

LONGMAN

LONGMAN GROUP LIMITED
Longman House,
Burnt Mill, Harlow, Essex CM20 2JE, England
and Associated Companies throughout the World.

First published 1977
Third impression 1983
ISBN 0 582 20537 9

Printed in Hong Kong by
Sheck Wah Tong Printing Press

Contents

To the Reader

Over 900 million people in the world are *Muslims*. A Muslim is someone who believes in the religion of *Islam*, which is an Arabic word meaning 'surrender.' The Islamic faith is based on the teachings of the prophet Muhammad who lived in the seventh century AD. He taught that there was only one God, and Muslims believe that Muhammad is his prophet, that is, the man chosen by God to bring people to understand his ways and to guide their lives. Whether or not we are Muslims it is right that we should know how and why this faith began.

So here is the story of Muhammad and how he changed the lives of his countrymen in Arabia. We shall see how they in turn carried their faith to distant places. We shall look at life in the cities of Damascus, Baghdad and Cairo and at what happened in the great days of the *caliphs* and the *sultans*. Most of the book will be about these central Islamic lands. Perhaps it will make you want to find out more about what is happening there today, or how the faith of Islam reached Pakistan and the east, or perhaps the story of Muslim times in Spain.

Today, when we use the term 'Islamic World' we usually mean to include all those countries where Islam is the chief religion. These include the East Indies, Pakistan, Iran, Turkey, parts of India and large areas of Africa. If we use the term 'Arab World' we usually mean those countries in the Middle East and North Africa where Arabic is the chief language. But, as you will find out in this book, many different peoples have moved over the Arab World. An Arab of today may be descended from parents who were Turkish, or Iranian, or African, or almost any other nationality of Europe, Asia or Africa. Some Arabs are Christian, particularly in Lebanon, Palestine and Egypt. But most follow the faith of Islam.

To find out how and where the faith of Islam began, we must start

The Kaba in Mecca

with the city of Mecca where Muhammad was born. In the picture above we are looking at the holy place in the middle of the city, towards which Muslims all over the world face whenever they pray.

Words printed in *italics* are listed in the Glossary on page 94.

1 *The Arabs and their Neighbours*

TOWNSMEN AND BEDOUIN

At the time we are thinking of, when Muhammad was born, Mecca was already an ancient Arab city. Some of its people were beginning to get rich through trading with countries to the north.

But most of the Arabs did not live in towns. Apart from anything else, there was not enough food and water for large numbers of people to live together. Some years there is no rain at all. There is never more in a year than many parts of the world get in one or two big storms. If you look around you, there is just sand or dry brown earth and rocks. The north-western part of Arabia is the most difficult to live in. In English it is sometimes called the Empty Quarter. The ancient Romans called it Arabia Deserta. It is the unkindest desert in the world.

Where water could be found, mostly in *oases* round the edges of the worst part of this desert, a little farming was possible. People could settle and build houses. But many had to live a wandering life. These were the *Bedouin*, always on the move with their sheep and goats, looking for land where the animals could find something to eat. Instead of fixed homes the Bedouin had tents, usually made of black cloth woven from goats' hair, with carpets on the ground to sit and lie on. The women had to pack away the tents when it was time to move on, and put them up again at the new site. The men looked after the animals.

Camels made this kind of life possible. They could go where the famous Arab horses could not. The horses were for luxury and for war: the camels were for living. Their broad feet and thick soles made them the only known animal able to carry the Bedouin and their loads across the desert lands. In places where the spring rain in February brought out the tender green shoots, the camels could rest and eat. For some weeks, in a good year, they put on weight and built up the fat in their humps. They could then live off this fat through the summer heats, with little food or water. When spring had gone and the young plants were dry and withered, there might be nothing for them to eat but leaves from the thorn trees along their route. They were able to feed on these without cutting their mouths on the sharp thorns. One travelling stranger in modern times was amazed at this. His Bedouin friends told him: 'The world is full of the wonderful works of God, and he has made every creature to his proper *livelihood*.'

Camels not only made it possible for the Bedouin to travel. They provided milk to drink, and their dung could be burnt to give heat. Sometimes one had to be killed, perhaps because it could not keep up with the others. Then the skin made good leather and the hump could be boiled down to produce fat for cooking. The flesh was used as food; even the bones were put to use: as tablets to write on or as arrows for war.

Today when people are asked where they come from, they usually answer with the name of the place where they were born or grew up in. In ancient times no Bedouin would do that. How could they, when they spent most of their time on the move? The important thing was not places but people. So they gave the names of their father and grandfather, and the larger group or tribe they belonged to. A wide and deep family feeling lay behind all they did. You could only survive the hard Bedouin life if you stuck together. Each supported the others in his group, knowing his name would be disgraced if he failed to help a relative in time of need. You could earn a good name by avenging members of your family if another group did them wrong, or by fighting bravely for your own tribe in a quarrel with another.

Townsmen did not depend on one another so much. In their daily life each had his own affairs to see to. There were

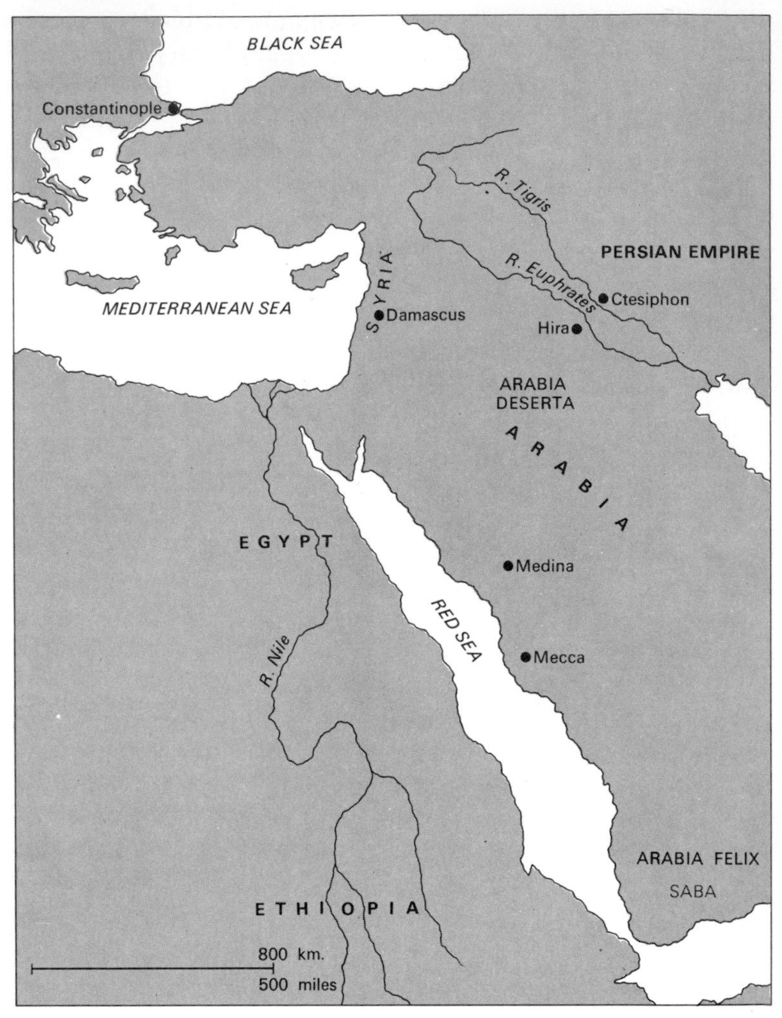

The Arabs and their neighbours

fewer hardships to keep folk together. You can imagine that townsmen and Bedouin did not always get on well. A townsman would never want to go back and share the hard, desert life. He would very likely fear that the Bedouin had their eye on his riches. And, as one Arab writer put it: 'Whenever a man's eye dwells on the goods of his neighbour his hand is apt to follow it.' All the same, the two had some important things in common. Most Bedouin had relatives who had made the change to a settled life, so they would share the same family feelings. To guests all Arabs were always full of welcome and generosity. For this the Arab world is still famous. Above all, townsmen and Bedouin shared the rich Arabic language.

SOUTHERN NEIGHBOURS

Far to the south the scene was very different. Here was Arabia Felix – fortunate Arabia – fortunate through its climate and the riches it produced. You can see on the map opposite the fertile parts in the south-west corner of the peninsula. There lived the people of Saba, to use their Bible name. Compared

An ancient tombstone from Arabia Felix. Can you guess what any of the people are doing?

with the hard living in the deserts of the north, theirs was a life of ease and prosperity. They grew the plants that produced the perfumes and spices people in the ancient world valued most. The Sabaeans also traded down the East African coast and across the sea to India, to bring gold, ivory, silks and gem stones. With these and their own precious spices, they would set out on camelback north-westward to the Mediterranean lands. These were the *caravans* – a word the Persians first used to describe a band of merchants, or *pilgrims*, travelling together for safety and survival. For safety? Many Bedouins would be glad of the chance to raid and rob them on the way. As for survival, nobody would travel the dry desert routes on his own without a helping hand in case of accident or illness.

THE EMPIRES TO THE NORTH: PERSIA AND THE BYZANTINES

By about AD 600 the Meccans themselves were beginning to take part in this trade. The leading tribe in the city were the Quraysh (pronounced Kraish). Twice a year they organised trading caravans with goods they had bought from the southern Arabians. Who were their customers?

Many were rich Persians in the lands along the banks of the Tigris and Euphrates rivers. The Persians' capital was then

The ruined palace at Ctesiphon

Ctesiphon, where their emperor Khusro I built a magnificent palace: he died in the year 579, when Muhammad was a boy. The part of his palace shown opposite is all that is left of the capital city. We are looking at the front wall and one of the huge vaults. Once there were two of these, built with bricks and standing over 30 metres high. Now the place is deserted except for the birds that perch on the highest bricks and glide over the ruins. As you can see from the map on page 8 Ctesiphon was on the other side of the Tigris from Arabia. The Meccan caravans went only as far as Hira, on their side of the Euphrates.

The Arabs' other northern neighbours – from Syria west and south to Egypt – were all subjects of the Byzantine emperor, who lived in Constantinople. In Khusro I's time this was the famous Justinian. You can read about him in another book in this series 'Constantinople and the Byzantines'. In their trading with the Byzantine lands the Meccans travelled

A sixth-century painting showing Christ and Saint Menas

to Damascus in Syria. The round journey from Mecca there and back often used to take five or six months, though it could be done in four.

PEOPLE OF THE BOOK

These other peoples had very different ideas about religion. There were the Jews, who were well known in Arabia, as there were a number of Jewish towns along the trading routes. The Jewish religion had once been strong in Saba. In Egypt and Syria Christianity was the religion of most people, as it was all over the Byzantine world. The picture on the previous page was painted in Egypt, probably about Muhammad's time. It shows Jesus Christ with his hand on the shoulder of Menas, an Egyptian saint.

While Jews and Christians believed there was one and only one God, many gods were worshipped in Mecca. But more than that, both Jews and Christians were People of the Book. The Jews had the five Books of Moses, the Christians had the New Testament. Here a man might look for guidance on what he should believe and how he should live his life. There were no books in Arabic which could give this help.

THE KABA

The most famous place of worship in Mecca was the *Kaba*. You can see a view of it on page 5 as it looks today. But it was old long before Muhammad was born. The Kaba itself, standing in the centre of the courtyard, was first built in the form of a simple cube – which the word Kaba means. In the beginning, Muslims believe, it was a holy place, holy to *Allah* – that is, God. But gradually it became a place of pilgrimage from all over Arabia, and every group of Arabs brought statues of their own gods to be worshipped. These were set in the courtyard round the Kaba. We are told there were well over three hundred of them. At the yearly festival Mecca was packed with visitors bringing prayers and gifts for their gods: food and wine, slaughtered animals, or sometimes necklaces and nose-rings. It was not only a religious occasion but a grand fair as well.

You could buy and sell gold and silver, the perfumes of the south, rich cloths and silks from Egypt and China – and slaves. There was singing and dancing, and plenty of wine to drink.

The Quraysh, the main tribe in the city, had the task and the privilege of looking after the Kaba. The time came when it needed complete rebuilding from the foundations. Four groups of men from different sections of the city were to do the work. Each set about collecting fresh stones and the rebuilding went ahead well until they reached the spot where the sacred black stone should be. The black stone had been sacred to the people of Mecca even before Muhammad's time. It is a *meteorite* which looks very different from other large stones found on the earth because it has a black crust around it. When it was found people knew nothing about meteorites, and they thought it was very strange and looked on it as something that had been sent from God. A bitter quarrel broke out between the groups over who should have the honour of lifting the stone into its place. It almost came to bloodshed. At last the oldest man there made a suggestion: the first person to come through the doorway into the courtyard of the Kaba should judge what must be done. They all agreed and settled down anxiously to wait.

The next to come in was somebody known to many of them already by a special name: al-Amin, 'the Trustworthy'. The story goes on:

> When he came near, they told him of the problem and he said, 'Bring me a cloak.' When they had brought one, he placed the black stone in it with his own hands, saying, 'Let every group take hold of a part of the cloak.' Then all of them lifted it together, and when they reached the spot, he placed it in position with his own hands, and the building was continued over it.

This man's real name was Muhammad.

2 *Muhammad and his Teachings*

THE LIFE OF THE PROPHET

'By the light of day, and by the fall of night, your Lord has not forsaken you. Did He not find you an orphan and give you shelter? Did he not find you in error and guide you? Did he not find you poor and enrich you?'

These words sum up Muhammad's life. He was born in Mecca in about 571 (by Christian dating). By birth he was a member of the leading tribe, the Quraysh. His father did not live to see him; and his mother died when he was very young, thus leaving him an orphan. When he was grown up, Muslims believe that he was guided from the 'error' of the old Arab ideas into speaking the word of the one God. After he got married he was not short of money. So he was 'enriched' in one way. But he never lived in *luxury*. He was promised by Allah that his reward would come in heaven after his earthly death: 'The life to come holds a richer prize for you than this present life.'

The two people who brought Muhammad up were his father's father and later one of his uncles, Abu Talib. As a boy he made the journey to Damascus in Abu Talib's company. After that, like many other young Meccans, he took to earning his living in the caravan trade. This is when he won his reputation for being trustworthy and truthful.

At that time there was a rich businesswoman in Mecca, called Khadija. She used to employ people to trade for her in return for a share in the profits. Through this she met Muhammad, and she sent him with one of the Syrian caravans on her behalf. On his return from Damascus, she offered to be his wife. His uncles arranged things with Khadija's father according to custom and they were married. He was twenty-five and she was forty. They had many children, four girls, and two (or some say three) boys. The boys died young but the girls all grew up to see the religion of Islam firmly founded. Muhammad and Khadija had a happy life together and it was only ended by Khadija's death, twenty-five years after their wedding. In the same year Abu Talib also died.

These two blows hit Muhammad very hard at a time when he badly needed help. 'After that,' in the words of an early writer of his life, '*calamities* followed because in losing his wife the apostle of Allah lost his faithful supporter in Islam. And in losing his uncle he lost his defender against the people.' What had such a man done to make enemies? Why should he need defending?

A few years after he had solved the dispute at the rebuilding of the Kaba, Muhammad had the most important experience of his life. As the same writer tells: 'When Muhammad was forty years old Allah sent him as a *prophet* of mercy to the people of the visible and of the invisible worlds, and to all mankind.' He had by now made a habit of spending some time in a cave on Mount Hira, a wild, rugged spot out in the desert near Mecca. There he had time to think in peace by himself. He could think of the troubles of his Arab countrymen and the old customs of the desert life. He could see that the people of Mecca no longer kept to the old ways of living. They were busy with their new-found trade. Some people were getting rich. Many were staying poor. Instead of everybody taking part in the life of the group, it was more a case of each man for himself. Perhaps the old ways did not suit city life, but there was nothing to take their place.

In this particular year, AD 610, Muhammad went to Mount Hira as usual. The story goes on:

> In the night the angel Gabriel came with the command of Allah. The *apostle* of Allah [that is, Muhammad] later said, 'He came while I was asleep and he said, "Read."

> I replied, "I cannot read." Then he pressed me in embrace till I thought I was dying; he released his hold and said, "Read." I replied, "I cannot read." And he pressed me again till I thought I was dying. Then he loosed his hold of me and said, "Read." I replied, "I cannot read." Once more he pressed me and said, "Read." Then I asked, "What shall I read?" Then he said, "Read in the name of the Lord thy *Creator*; who *created* man from a drop of blood. Read this thy Lord is the most *bountiful*, who taught by means of the pen, taught man what he knew not." Accordingly I recited these words, and he had finished his task and departed from me. I felt as if words had been *graven* on my heart. Afterwards I went out, and when I was on the centre of the mountain, I heard a voice from heaven, saying, "O Muhammad! Thou art the prophet of Allah, and I am Gabriel."

Muhammad returned to his wife very puzzled. What could this mean? Khadija comforted him, saying she hoped he would indeed be the prophet of Allah, speaking the words of God to his countrymen. For a while nothing further happened. Then Muhammad had another vision of the angel Gabriel coming to him. He spoke some more words to him: words of comfort, words of encouragement, words outlining his task and suggesting the ways he should fulfil it. He was told to go out and '*declare* the goodness of the Lord', to say what he had heard and to pray. In particular he was to pray that God would go on speaking to him.

This was the beginning of his preaching. First it was just Khadija and their children, then a few friends, who made the statement of faith 'There is no god but God [that is, Allah], and Muhammad is his messenger'. Others began to join them. This small group of the faithful, as they called themselves, was known as the Companions, a title of great honour in the world of Islam. The first three Companions were Ali his cousin (who later married his daughter Fatima); Zayd, a former slave of Khadija's, whom Muhammad had adopted as his son; and Abu Bakr, his greatest friend, who kept a shop and sold cloth.

Others who joined the group in those early days were Uthman, a noble merchant, and Umar, a brave fighter. All of them served as Muhammad's constant advisers.

As his preaching spread, Muhammad ran into trouble, particularly from the Quraysh. It was bad enough for them to be asked to give up all their 'gods' and follow just one. They couldn't believe this unimportant-looking person really knew. 'How is it that he eats and walks about the market-squares? Why has no angel been sent down with him to warn us? Why has no treasure been given him, no garden to provide his food?' But Muhammad taught things that hurt the wealthy traders even more. 'The unbelievers say: "We have been given more wealth and children than the faithful. Surely we shall never be punished." Neither your riches nor your children shall bring you nearer to Us.' (that is to God). God, said Muhammad, did not favour rich people.

But to others, both among the townsmen and the Bedouin, Muhammad seemed to offer something more than the old tribal life. There you were judged by your wealth, what you owned, and the size and prosperity of your family. What your fellow-tribesmen thought of you was what counted. Under Muhammad's teaching it was for you to decide, on your own, because all men came before God on the day of judgment. Then money would be no help to you, for that was when 'men's hidden thoughts were laid open and their Lord would on that day know all that they had done'. Those that believed in Allah and did what was right would be forgiven their sins and admitted to gardens watered by running streams, where they would dwell for ever. But those that disbelieved would be the heirs of Hell and abide therein for ever.

Though a few of the wealthier folk listened, the poor and the slaves were the ones who really welcomed the new teacher. The opposition started with people just laughing at Muhammad and his followers at their prayers. Then it came to stone-throwing and violence. The faithful went in fear of their lives. A party of about eighty crossed the Red Sea as refugees to the Christian kingdom of Ethiopia. They were made welcome by the Christians as fellow-believers in one God.

This happened in about 615. Four years later came Muhammad's 'year of sorrow' in which his wife and his uncle both died. Until Khadija's death he had no other wife: afterwards he married many – about eleven altogether. But it seems they did not bring him real happiness. It was always Khadija he remembered. It was always she who was there by his side to help in his early struggles. Abu Talib had never made the statement of faith. But with true Arab family loyalty he firmly supported his nephew against all his attackers.

Until Abu Talib died, none of the Quraysh dared to harm Muhammad personally. After that it was different. The new head of his tribe was firmly against the teachings of Islam. For some days Muhammad had to leave Mecca, otherwise he would almost certainly have been killed. This was the most bitter time in his life. He knew it was through him that the faithful had joined Islam, and now he could do nothing to protect them.

THE HIJRA AND AFTER

Help came from an unexpected place. Among visitors to the great festival at Mecca one year was a party of pilgrims from Medina. This was a city nearly 400 kilometres to the north, along the road to Damascus. It so happened that these men heard Muhammad's teaching. They welcomed it gladly. But more than that, when they got home to Medina they found willing listeners as well. Their fellow-townsmen were going through a bad time of fights and quarrels between rival groups, and the teaching of Islam seemed to offer a way out. The next year, a group of twelve there who had made the statement of faith came to meet Muhammad and promised their help. For this, the faithful in Mecca called these men of Medina the Helpers – another proud title in the Islamic world.

The year after that – 622 by Christian dating – is the greatest in the history of Islam. It happened like this. More than seventy Helpers met Muhammad in secret and made a solemn promise. If need be, they would actually fight against his enemies. But the news leaked out to the Quraysh and the Helpers were really in trouble. They nearly all managed to reach home safely. Gradually Muhammad made arrangements for his Meccan followers to leave for Medina and join their new friends. In small groups over a hundred men got away. The Quraysh were upset over these new developments, and they decided to kill Muhammad. They surrounded his house. Most of the companions had left Mecca. Among those who were still with Muhammad in Mecca were Abu Bakr and Ali. Abu Bakr had bought two camels and was keeping them ready for just this emergency. One night he and Muhammad slipped out of the back of his house. Ali was told to stay and look after their families: Muhammad also handed over to him all the valuables people had kept with him to be returned to them after his departure. Muhammad and Abu Bakr waited in a cave near the city and planned their departure. First came Abu Bakr's son to tell them that the Quraysh were offering a hundred camels to anyone who would bring Muhammad back. Then on the third day, when the excitement had died down a little, came Abu Bakr's daughter with food and their guide with the camels. Muhammad and Abu Bakr set out by a roundabout route: eight days later they were safe in Medina with the others.

This was called the Hijra (pronounced Hijra) – the parting from the Quraysh, his own people. It meant that Muhammad was no longer one of them. Those Meccans who were with him in Medina shared the proud title of *Emigrants*. So we can remember these three – the Companions, the Helpers and the Emigrants. All have a very special place in the story of their religion. They followed Muhammad when things were bad and before he was famous. They risked a lot to do so.

Some years afterwards, the Companions realised that the journey to Medina was really the starting point. Instead of always facing the chance of being beaten up or even killed, they were now free to carry on their lives in the way Muhammad taught them. They no longer had to suffer in silence. Thus the time of the Hijra became for them the year 1, and all later events were dated from that.

At the time of the Hijra, Muhammad was just over fifty. He had ten years to live. By the time of his death in AD 632 most people in Arabia had accepted the one God and the teachings of Muhammad as God's prophet. In Mecca the old statues and images had gone. It was the holy city and the centre of Islam. How had this been achieved? There were a few battles against the Quraysh and their friends, but they were very small ones. In a modern war they would hardly be called battles at all. The total number of people killed in all these battles was about a hundred. Some of the Jews who opposed Muhammad were killed and many more driven out of the Arab cities, one of which was Mecca. But force and violence did not make people follow him. The main thing was the power of his teaching and the way he was able to win men's hearts. Before the Helpers made their promise, they asked Muhammad what their reward would be if they kept faith with him in the face of all misfortune. '*Paradise*' he replied. This was a promise of a life of perfect happiness in the next world after death. It made Bedouin and townsmen ready to fight with him for the cause of Islam. Life in this world, too, seemed to be richer. Before this, they said, God had spoken only to Jews and Christians. Now He had chosen as His prophet one of themselves, speaking their own Arabic language. They could look beyond the narrow life of their tribal group with its endless quarrels, and feel proud to be a member of a new and wider world.

What about Muhammad's personal life? In reading about Muhammad today, two things stand out. One is the way he considered other people. It might be a very small thing, like the time he refused his supper, which had *garlic* in it. His hosts were very alarmed when they went in to find the dish untouched, and asked the reason. He replied: 'I found in it the smell of this plant, and I am a man who has close contact with others. But you may eat it.' Or there was the problem of choosing a place to live in Medina from the many offered to him. How could he choose one without upsetting all the other house-owners? He let his camel choose, and said: 'Allow my camel to go where she will, because she is guided by Allah.'

The Islamic Calendar

Muhammad actually got to Medina on 24 September 622 (by Christian dating). After his death Umar decided there should be one way of reckoning dates all over the Muslim world. He used the old Arab calendar. 16 July 622 was the first day of the Arab year in which the Hijra took place. So this became the first day of the Islamic year 1. Just as Christian years are described as AD (Anno Domini latin for the year of the Lord), so the Islamic years are AH (Anno Hegirae – in the year of the Hijra).

The Islamic year is a little shorter than the Christian one. For example, 1392 AH began on 16 February 1972, and 1393 AH began on 4 February 1973. This is because the Christian year is based on the time it takes for the earth to travel round the sun. But the Islamic year goes by the movement of the moon and is made up of twelve lunar months. The best-known one to non-Muslims is the ninth month, *Ramadan*, the month of fasting. A month starts when the new moon appears.

Here are some of the main events in Muhammad's life.

AD (Anno Domini)		(Anno Hegirae) AH
571	Muhammad's birth	
595	His marriage to Khadija	
610	About then, Muhammad started his teaching	
615	Some of the faithful migrate to Ethiopia	
619	Death of Khadija and his uncle Abu Talib	
622	The Hijra	1
623	Battle of Badr: Muslims defeat Meccan force	2
624	Battle of Uhud: Muslims defeated by Meccans	3
630	The Muslims take Mecca	9
632	Muhammad's death	11

The other is the humble way he lived. He was always thinking of the people who had nothing in this world. So long as he had anything he would share it with them. In this he practised his own preaching: 'Send good works ahead of you for the benefit of your souls! . . . He who can give even a little piece of date, and does so, will help to shade his face from the fire of hell.' (Remember that dates, from date-palms, were one of the main foods of desert people.)

THE QURAN (pronounced Koran)

After Muhammad had his first vision on Mount Hira, there were many times when the word of God came to him. Muslims believe that what he said then did not come from his own thoughts: he was speaking what God revealed to him. It happened for the rest of his life, both in Mecca and later in his house in Medina. It could happen even in the middle of a battle. In all this, he thought of himself as following the prophets and religious leaders of ancient times, like Abraham, men sent by God to guide the human race in what they should believe and what they should do.

The whole collection of what came to Muhammad at these particular times makes up the book called the *Quran*. Some he may have put in writing himself. At other times the Companions wrote down the words as he spoke them. They used anything that was convenient to write on – palm leaves, flat stones, the bones of animals. Others learnt long pieces by heart. They could then recite them to people. Zayd, Muhammad's secretary, made a collection and gave all he had to Abu Bakr, when Muhammad died. But, as you can imagine, it was difficult to be sure it was complete, or that all the items were really what Muhammad had said. Soon there were four different books, all a little different from each other. The Quran as we have it now was put together a few years after Muhammad's death by a group of learned experts, Zayd among them. They studied all the differences in the four books and finally decided what was correct, and what should be left out. There have been no changes since. On the next page

A leaf from one of the oldest known copies of the Quran

is a photograph of a leaf from one of the oldest known copies of the Quran in the world. It comes from Arabia and dates from about a century after Muhammad's death. It was copied on goatskin in an early kind of Arabic writing. By contrast you can see on page 25 a page from the Quran copied in Nigeria about a hundred years ago. Sometimes a copy was bound up to make a single book. Sometimes it made a number of volumes and a special *chest* was needed to keep them all in. The wooden Quran chest shown on page 25 is for a set of this kind. There are two compartments inside, each holding fifteen volumes. It was carved in Egypt more than 700 years ago.

At the beginning of this chapter and in the account of Muhammad's teaching (on page 16) you read pieces from a modern translation of the Quran into English. From a translation you can indeed find out the facts of Muhammad's teaching. But reading it in another language is quite different from hearing it in Arabic. Those who know it say it has a special beauty which no other Arabic has. Because of this, the kind of Arabic in which the Quran was written is still in use today. Muslims from countries far apart may not always understand each other's modern Arabic: this can be different from country to country. But using the Arabic of the Quran they can talk with each other.

THE FIVE PILLARS

Muhammad himself said that Islam was built on five pillars. To put it another way, a Muslim has five main duties in supporting his faith.

1 The first is the STATEMENT OF FAITH. To be a Muslim, the first thing you must do is to declare the belief, in front of *witnesses*, that there is no other god but Allah and that Muhammad is his prophet. We read earlier how the first Companions – and later the Helpers from Medina – made this statement of faith. Muslims believe that there were prophets before Muhammad, and accept Jesus as one of them. But they believe that because Jesus was a man, he cannot be God. That is the chief difference between what Christians and Muslims think about Jesus.

2 PRAYER. There are five times for daily prayer which Muslims must keep: at dawn, at midday, in the afternoon, at sunset, and later at night. Muhammad prayed far more often, but 'prayer is heavy – people are weak'. Friday is particularly the day to go to the *mosque* for prayer. 'Believers,' says the Quran, 'when you are summoned to Friday prayers, hasten to the remembrance of Allah and cease your trading.' On that day, the weekly holiday, the normal midday prayer is replaced: there are no priests in Islam, but a leader called the *imam* preaches a sermon. Then he leads the congregation in prayers, facing as always towards Mecca. Any Muslim can lead the prayer. It is suggested the more learned and pious a person is, the greater is his right to lead the prayer.

3 ALMSGIVING. We have seen what Muhammad did when he saw somebody needed help. How much help should people be ready to give? In the words of the Quran: 'They ask you what

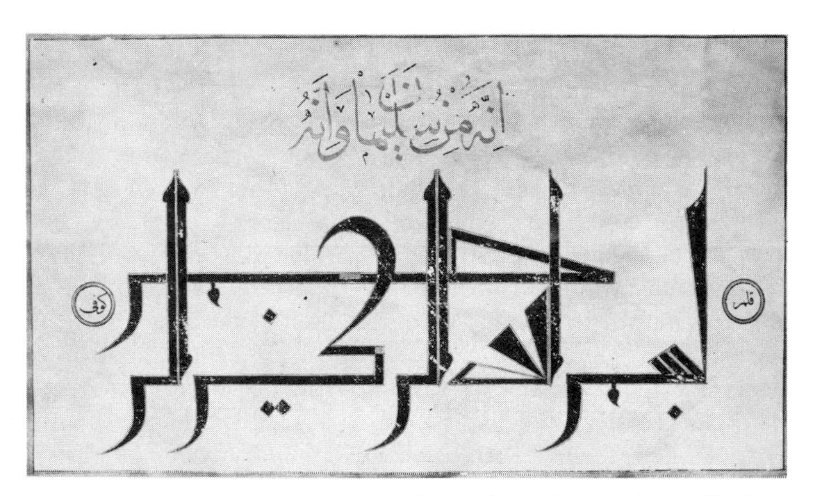

A page from a Quran copied in Nigeria

A Quran chest

they should give in *alms*. Say: "What ever you can spare."'
Later it was a rule that Muslims should give one fortieth, $2\frac{1}{2}$ per cent, of their wealth. It became a kind of tax, on top of any other help people gave of their own accord. Today things are more as they were in Muhammad's time. It is a matter of each person making up his mind 'what he can spare'.

4 FASTING. Muslims over the age of twelve must *fast* from dawn to sunset every day throughout the month of Ramadan. (This was the month in which Muhammad had his first vision on Mount Hira.) During this time you cannot even take a sip of water, however hot the weather is. How do you tell when the dawn has really come? The Quran says: 'Eat and drink until you can tell a white thread from a black one.' The fast is something for poor and rich alike. It can show that you have the power to rule yourself. It is also a reminder that all human beings are equal in the eyes of God. The end of Ramadan is celebrated with Id-ul-Fitr, a day of feasting, prayer and thanksgiving. For the children it means new clothes and family presents. For all it means visiting friends and exchanging greetings. The other great festival of Islam is Id-ul-Adha, which comes at the end of the Meccan pilgrimage, two months and nine days after Id-ul-Fitr.

5 THE HAJJ. This brings us to the fifth pillar: the duty of every Muslim at least once in his lifetime, if he can afford it, to make the *pilgrimage* – the hajj. This is the duty that brings over a million and a half Muslims in the last month of the year every year to the city of Mecca. Once, by camel and on foot, it was for some a journey of months or sometimes years. Even with air travel it means, for many people, being away from home for three weeks. Just as the earlier pilgrims hundreds of years ago, the pilgrim of today visits the places where Muhammad once taught: with fellow-Muslims from across the world he reaches the Kaba itself.

These are the five great duties. Have you noticed that, except in some ways for the fourth, all the pillars are about things you ought to do – not things you should stop doing? There are three things particularly which non-Muslims often think of as part of the Muslim way of life. These are not among the five pillars. Two are rules of the 'don't' kind. Most non-Muslims know that Muslims are not allowed to eat pork or bacon. In Muhammad's time pig meat was often very unhealthy, and so this was a sensible rule. Today when in most countries there are strict health rules for farmers and butchers and pork is safe to eat, why not eat it? Muslims would say that controlling your eating habits is one of the clearest signs that you are a Muslim. This is specially important if you are living in a country where Muslims are a *minority*. Give up this rule, they say, and soon you will give up a great deal more: in time you stop practising the rest of the Muslim way of life. Another well-known rule is the one against taking alcohol: it is interesting to read what the Quran says on this. As usual, God is speaking to Muhammad: 'They ask you about drinking and gambling. Say: "There is great harm in both, although they have some benefit for men; but their harm is far greater than their benefit." '

The third thing is one that leads to a lot of misunderstanding between Muslims and others. Many non-Muslims know that a Muslim man can have up to four wives at the same time. They often do not know the other rule, that if he cannot look after them all equally well, he should keep to one. In fact all this goes back to the old times in Arabia when there were sometimes more women than men because of death in war: most Muslims stick to the one-husband-one-wife family these days. But a bigger question for many people is what to think when they read in the Quran that 'men have a status above women' (that is, men are more important than women). In some countries (both Muslim and non-Muslim) it looks so to outsiders. In others, you will be told that this is no longer true, or that it was never true. But in all Muslim countries there is a common feeling that however 'equal' men and women are, they have different parts to play in life – that some jobs are more suitable for women and some for men. One thing everyone agrees on is that, by teaching as he did, Muhammad gave women a better position in life than they had had before.

3 *The Rule of the Companions*

ISLAM'S NEW LEADERS

Not long after returning to his house in Medina from a final pilgrimage, Muhammad fell sick. During his final illness he lay in the room of Aisha, the wife he was closest to at the end. She was the daughter of Abu Bakr. He died in her room and was buried in Medina.

On the morning of his death he appeared at the doorway as he tried to come out and join in the morning prayer. The people thought he must be getting better. But this effort was too much for him and he died later the same day. In their grief and shock at losing the person at the centre of their lives, they asked each other the great question – what next? They could hardly take in what had happened. To many, and particularly those farther away from Medina, it looked like the end of Islam. They had made their promise to Muhammad. On his death they felt free to look elsewhere for a leader. Some nearly went back to worshipping the old gods.

In Medina the leading Companions met to decide what to do. Muhammad had not actually named anybody to succeed him, and there was argument between the Helpers and the Emigrants. Then Umar made a sign that he would serve under Abu Bakr, and the rest followed. Finally Abu Bakr spoke: 'I am appointed to govern you, although I am not the best of you. If I act well, you must aid me, and if I act unjustly you must correct me. Truth is faithfulness and *falsehood* is treachery! Obey me as long as I obey Allah and His prophet! But should I rebel against Allah and His prophet you will owe me no obedience! Rise to your prayers and may Allah have mercy on you.'

Abu Bakr did not rule as a prophet. To the Muslims there could be no prophet after Muhammad. He was the first khalifa (in English, caliph), which means successor – the one to come after the apostle of God.

Among the weapons in the Topkapi Museum in Istanbul (the modern name of Constantinople) are the four swords you see here. The *hilts* and *scabbards* were made much later, but

The swords of the four caliphs

the blades inside are believed to be the swords of the four Companions who ruled the growing world of Islam for the next thirty years. Under these four, Arab armies burst out of their desert homelands. They took power in all the countries from Egypt in the west to Persia in the east, and away to Syria in the north as you can see from the map on page 34. Later we shall see how this was done.

Abu Bakr's main work was to make it clear to all the people of Arabia that Islam had not died with Muhammad. With some of the Arab tribes this meant fighting. General Khalid was in charge of this – the Sword of Allah, as Muhammad called him. Very soon all the Arabs had accepted that they were still members of the Muslim state. Abu Bakr himself stayed mostly in Medina and was busy with his religious duties.

He died dressed in the clothes of a poor man to meet his God, and was buried beside Muhammad.

THE RULE OF THE COMPANIONS

AD (Anno Domini)		AH (Anno Hegirae)
632–634	Abu Bakr	11–13
634–644	Umar	13–23
644–656	Uthman	23–35
656–661	Ali	35–41

In books about Islam, dates are sometimes given in both ways: the year Umar became caliph could be shown as 13/634.

As Abu Bakr had asked, the Companions chose Umar to follow him. In his ten-year reign, Umar was the one who took the power of Islam so far outside Arabia. He was a great man and as a fighter he was greatly feared. He also did much to plan how the Arabs would rule the newly taken lands. He is remembered, too, for fixing the starting year of the Muslim calendar in the way we read in the last chapter. When he was a little over sixty he was killed by a young Persian. Like Abu Bakr, he was buried by the side of the prophet.

The third caliph was Uthman, already quite old when chosen. He was a kind and generous person. It was he who circulated the authorised version of the Quran throughout the Muslim realm. He will always be honoured by Muslims for this. But as a ruler he could not find the answers to the problems of his time, and made many enemies. His end was pitiful, for he was stabbed to death by fellow-Muslims while actually reading the Quran. Its leaves were soaked in his blood. The fourth and last Companion to be caliph was Ali, the husband of Muhammad's daughter Fatima. He too, was killed by another Muslim, as we shall see.

Muhammad knew there would be fighting among his

followers when he was dead. Could he have foreseen anything as grim as this?

DAR AL-HARB – THE PLACE OF WAR

Ever since the Helpers had made their promise to stand by Muhammad, this oath had bound men to fight, if necessary, against unbelievers. From this grew the idea of holy war: in Arabic, jihad. In the minds of these early Muslims the world was divided into two areas. Dar al-Islam was the home or place of Islam, where there should be peace between all peoples, whatever their race or religion and wherever they came from. The lands outside Islam were Dar al-Harb, the place of war. Muhammad and Abu Bakr had made the whole of Arabia Dar al-Islam. After that the Arabs, and particularly the Bedouin fighters, turned their eyes to the richer lands around them. Soon their armies were moving across the deserts.

You will remember the Arabs' northern neighbours, how they were ruled by the Persian king with his capital at Ctesiphon, or by the Byzantines from far-off Constantinople. During Muhammad's lifetime these two powers had fought each other in a long and bitter war. In the end the Byzantines had won: indeed the Quran had foretold that this was the will of Allah. But neither side had any strength left. At first none of their leaders noticed the new power of Islam. Then they hardly believed these poor rough people from the desert could do anything to them. So it was, that when Khalid led his army across the Syrian desert in the year 14/635, he could take Damascus from the Byzantines. Two years later the Arab generals were ruling nearly all Syria.

In Jerusalem the leader of the Christian church there had to face the Arab forces. Like everybody else in that holy city, he knew what to expect whenever a foreign army took over – killing, burning, stealing. It had happened many times in Jerusalem's history. But this was different. In his richest robes as a *patriarch* of the Byzantine church he went out to ask for mercy. He was amazed to see before him the caliph Umar himself, in the dress of a poor pilgrim. Taking it in turns with his servant to ride, he had come across the Syrian desert.

Umar asked the patriarch to take him to the holy places in the city, which he did. When they reached the Church of the Holy Sepulchre the Christians invited Umar to say his prayers with them. But Umar said that if he did so it would encourage his followers to turn the church into a mosque. Instead, he moved right to the end of the main part of the church to pray. There is now a mosque on the site where he did this. Because the caliph and the patriarch believed they were praying to the same God, they were able to make a peaceful agreement together.

Here is the beginning of the treaty they made, in 17/638: 'In the name of Allah, the Merciful, the Compassionate. This is the *covenant* which Umar Ibn al-Khattab, the servant of Allah, the commander of the faithful, grants to the people of the Holy House. He grants them security of their lives, their possessions, their churches and crosses...'

Many Christian cities were taken in this way. There was fighting if the people resisted. Otherwise they were treated as People of the Book. In many places the new Arab rulers were welcomed. They made non-Muslims pay taxes, but less than the Byzantine emperors had asked for. This was true in Egypt most of all. There the Byzantines were hated. Apart from the heavy taxes, the Egyptians were not allowed to be Christians in the way they wanted. The Byzantines were always accusing them of having wrong beliefs. In 20/641 the Byzantines governor made peace with another Muslim general, Amr. The Byzantines never ruled Egypt again. This was a serious loss for them: every year they had taken the Egyptian wheat crop to feed all the hungry mouths in Constantinople.

Other Arab armies were moving into the empire of Persia. Here there was much fiercer fighting. In 15/636 they won a big battle on the road to Hira. Now there was nothing to stop them taking Ctesiphon itself, and all its treasures. Arab writers tell of a huge carpet in the great hall of the palace. (This is the noble ruin in the picture on page 11.) It seems to have been nearly a third the size of a football pitch today. It was woven to look like a garden. The earth was of gold thread, the paths of silver. Lawns, flowers and fruit were of precious stones, and through it all ran streams made of pearls. All this was torn to pieces and shared among the soldiers. The Persian armies fought again, but by 21/642 it was all over. The Persian empire was at an end.

A tenth-century pen drawing of an Arab horseman

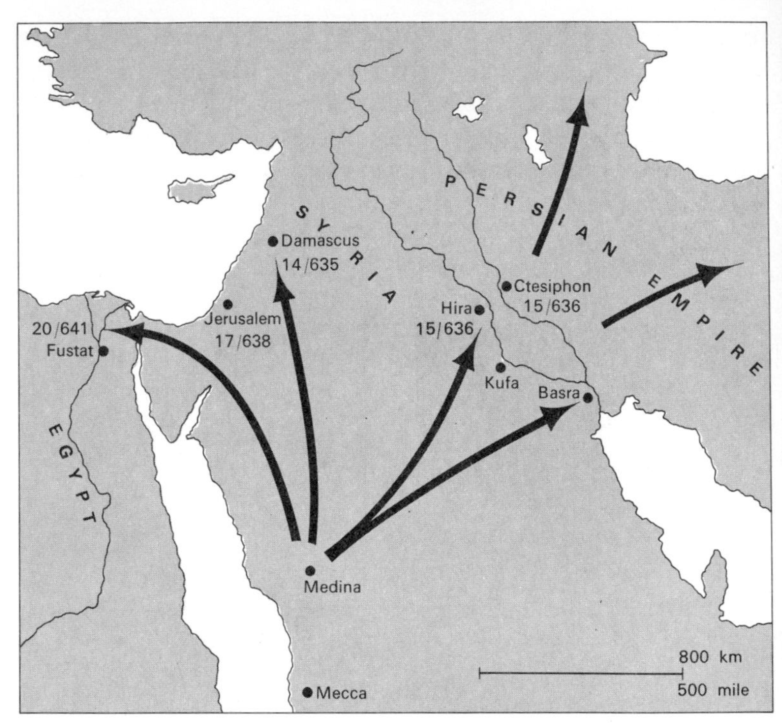

Early Muslim conquests. The arrows show the directions in which the Muslim armies went out from Medina at different times to conquer the surrounding areas

NEW WAYS OF LIVING

What did the Arabs feel, particularly the Bedouin soldiers? First they must have been filled with wonder at what they had done. They were no longer forced to lead a wretched life in the harsh deserts. Under their new faith they had been able to bury tribal quarrels and come together. The jihad had carried them to fertile lands, great riches and the promise of more to come.

Even the Arab armies could not be on the move all the time. They made camps in the new lands of Islam. Some of these gradually grew into new towns. The first three are shown on the map above: Fustat (just south of the present city of Cairo), Kufa and Basra. What was life there like, when the men were not away fighting? They mostly lived with their families in

Bedouin tents or simple buildings of sun baked bricks. There was strange food to get used to. When they first saw the thin flat bread of these lands, it looked to them more like sheets of paper for writing on. There were sweet fruits, beans and green vegetables, and more meat. But it was still not a life of luxury. Muhammad had always taught people to avoid having too much of anything, because it made you greedy. As in all they did, there were special rules at meals. First you had to know it was God who provided the food. Secondly you must be satisfied with whatever food was given. And then you should pray, saying 'in the name of God' before the meal, and 'to God be thanks' when you had finished. There was no school as we know it. When Arab fathers asked how to train their sons in the new lands, the caliph Umar said: 'Teach your boys how to swim and how to shoot with the bow. Teach them to ride a horse and to know and love poetry.'

The centre of town life was the mosque. Nowadays we think of mosques, like churches, as places of worship. In those early days of Islam people did not see religion and politics as separate things. Muhammad's house in Medina was a general meeting place for his followers as well as a place for teaching and prayer. So it was in the new lands. The mosque was often next to the governor's house. Here he could discuss things and announce important decisions. It took the place of a law court today. It was the first Islamic school, just as the Quran was the first textbook.

Sometimes the Muslims took over a Christian church, or part of it, and made it a mosque. In a new town they had to put up a special building. At first these were of a very simple kind, like the one Amr built at Fustat. This was only about thirty metres long and fifteen wide. The low roof was of palm branches to give shade from the sun. It was held up by palm trunks.

How did people know when it was time for prayer? There was much discussion about this in Muhammad's lifetime. Should they blow a horn like the Jews, or ring bells like some of the Christians? The decision was – neither. Instead a leader made a call to prayer in a loud voice. This is what he called out. 'God is the greatest. I give witness that there is none to worship except God. I give witness that Muhammad is God's apostle. Come to prayer. Come to security. There is no other God but God.'

The first to chant this call, the first *muezzin*, as such a person is named, was an African, Bilal. One of Muhammad's earliest followers, he had been tortured for holding his beliefs. He was the original muezzin in Medina until Muhammad's death. But from then he would not call, until the taking of Jerusalem six years later. There he was in Umar's party and his well-loved voice was heard again. He would stand anywhere his voice could be heard clearly, perhaps on a flat rooftop. Later special towers were built for the muezzin to call from. These are the *minarets* which are one of the clear signs of a mosque today. There are three other things a mosque needs. First there must be a fountain usually outside, so that people can wash before praying. Then inside the mosque itself there must be a *mihrab*: this is a place in the wall marking the direction of Mecca so that everybody knows where to turn when saying their prayers. Lastly there must be a *minbar*, or pulpit: this is where the imam gives the sermon at the midday prayer on Fridays. Artists and craftsmen all over the Muslim world have done some of their finest work producing these four things. There are pictures of them later in this book.

But all this lay in the future. In the days of the Companions Muslims did not think about grand buildings. Muhammad's teaching had been quite different. In the mosque in Medina there was a special place for the very poor and the very old or handicapped. Some of them had no other place to stay. Everything they ate came from the gifts of other believers, including Muhammad himself. To him they were 'the *fragile* ones', those who needed all the help of their fellow men. The first caliphs followed much of his way of life. They, too, had sat in the mosque with the fragile ones. All believers were to them equal under God. Even though Islam was now becoming a large empire they remained simple men.

4 Damascus and the Umayyads

A BREAK WITH THE PAST

The Muslim leaders could not live at peace among themselves. Nor did they go on ruling from the old cities of Arabia where Islam began. Ali, the last of the Companions to be caliph, left Medina to make a new capital in Kufa and never went back. He knew he had to stay in Kufa and face his enemies who were at Basra nearby. How could such a respected man, one of Muhammad's very earliest followers, have enemies among Muslims? These were the people who blamed him for not doing enough to punish Uthman's murderers.

But soon it became a deeper struggle. Should Ali be caliph at all? On one side were his supporters: they thought he had a special claim to be leader because he was married to Muhammad's daughter. Many others argued that this was wrong, but they could not agree on who should be caliph instead. So things stood until the year 40/660, when the governor of Syria, called Muawiya, refused to recognise the new Caliph Ali. He was a member of the Umayyad family and a relative of the dead Uthman. Wars were fought between the supporters of Ali and Muawiya, ending in uneasiness. The next year, Ali himself was killed with a blow from a poisoned dagger as he stood in the mosque in Kufa. After this, Muawiya was accepted as caliph by most of the Arabs, and members of his family were caliphs after him. So began the Umayyad dynasty which ruled the Muslim world for nearly a hundred years.

This was not the end of the matter. The Umayyads made sure Ali's sons were killed, but Ali's followers kept to their belief that the caliph should always be somebody from his family: they

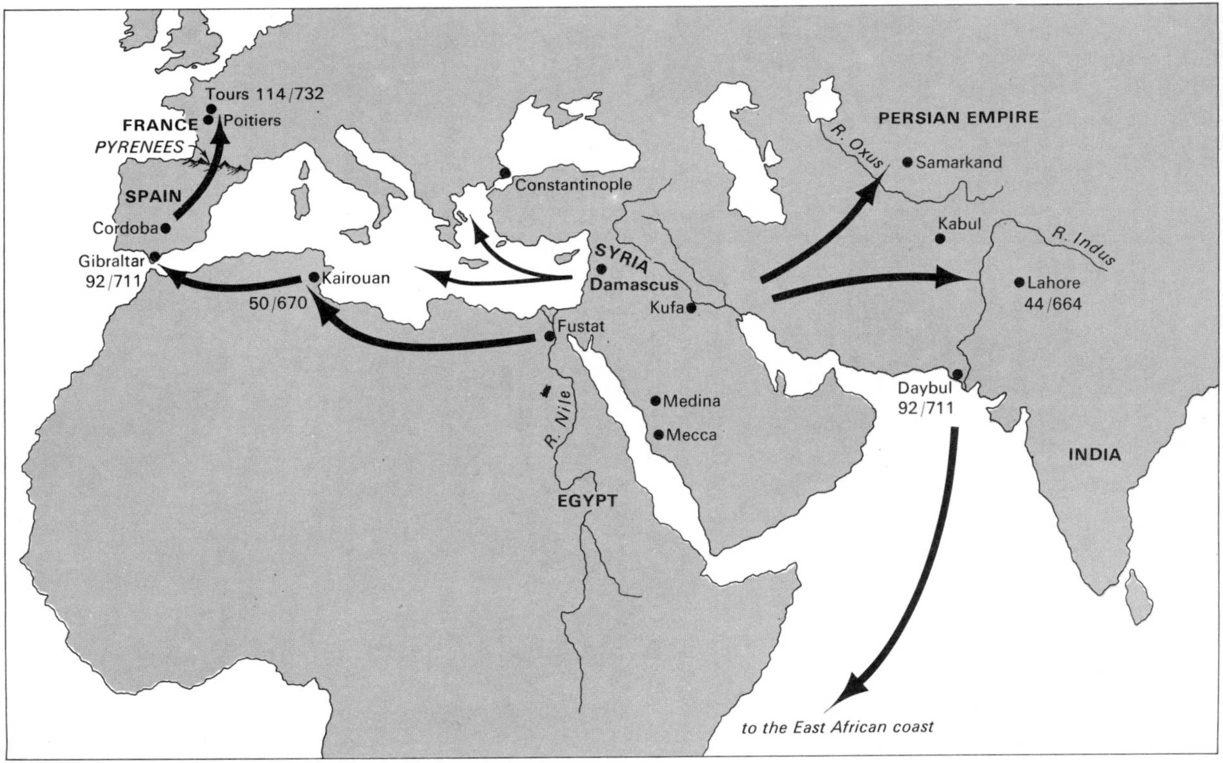

Tours 114/732
FRANCE
Poitiers
PYRENEES
SPAIN
Cordoba
Gibraltar
92/711
Kairouan
50/670
Constantinople
SYRIA
Damascus
Kufa
Fustat
R. Nile
EGYPT
Medina
Mecca
PERSIAN EMPIRE
R. Oxus
Samarkand
Kabul
R. Indus
Lahore
44/664
Daybul
92/711
INDIA
to the East African coast

are called Shiites – members of the Shia, the party of Ali. Others became known as Sunnis, thinking of themselves as true followers of the Sunna – the words and actions of Muhammad. This difference has lasted ever since.

The Umayyads made Damascus their capital. With this came another change. They did not follow the example of the Companions with their simple way of living. They did not sit with the fragile ones. They lived as kings of this world and Damascus lay at the centre of their huge empire. For the Arab armies rolled on, and under the Umayyads reached their farthest limits, from the Atlantic Ocean to the borders of China. The map opposite tells us more about this. In the east, one of Muawiya's generals got as far as Lahore. In the fiftieth year of Islam (AD 670) another built a new army town at Kairouan, now in Algeria. Soon all north Africa was part of Islam and Kairouan became its chief city.

Apart from Muawiya himself, the two Umayyad caliphs remembered for spreading Arab power are Abd al-Malik and his son Al-Walid I. The map shows some of the famous places their armies took in the east, whose peoples now joined the world of Islam. You can look for them in a modern atlas and see which countries they are in today. You will probably find the River Oxus under its modern name, Amu Darya: north of it lived peoples we have not met before in this book – the Turks. They were not yet settled in the country now called Turkey: we shall be hearing more of them. You may not find Daybul at all in your atlas. After the Arabs took it in the year 92/711 it became a great port, and from there the first Arab traders sailed to the coast of East Africa.

In the same year, right across in the west, a young general, Tariq, with a few thousand soldiers, crossed the straits between Africa and Europe. At that point there was a jabal – the Arabic word for a rocky hill. We now call this Gibraltar. Can you see how it got its name? The Arabs swept on, and soon Spain was part of their empire. They made Cordoba its chief city. In the hundredth year of Islam they were across the Pyrenees mountains and into France. Their advancing armies got nearly as far as Tours and Poitiers. Why did they get no further? In France they met a strong enemy for the first time: this was Charles Martel, who turned them back after a battle in the year 114/732. But in any case the Arab armies were now a very long way from home. There were too few of them, and they were not happy in these cold northern lands.

The Arabs had gone so far and taken so much. But the largest and richest city in the world, Constantinople, they could not take. They had built a great navy. For four years in Muawiya's time and again in Sulayman's they surrounded the city. The Byzantines stood firm behind their huge land and sea walls, and in the end drove the Arab ships away.

FAMOUS UMAYYAD CALIPHS

	AH	AD
Muawiya	40–60	660–680
Civil wars, during which the Kaba itself was burnt down		
Abd al-Malik	65–86	685–705
Al-Walid I	86–96	705–715
Hisham	105–125	724–743

THE GREAT BUILDERS

Constantinople was the world's richest city, but to Muslims their own capital Damascus was the most beautiful. It is also the oldest. People have been living there longer than in any other town in the world. When Muawiya made it his capital, it was already about four thousand years old. To Christians it is famous as the place where Paul had become a Christian in the days of the Roman empire. It has always been a green and fertile place, a great garden lying on the edge of the desert stretching away to the east. Here the Umayyads reigned, while their armies were reaching out to unknown and distant lands.

At first they did not care much what their buildings looked

A desert palace of the Umayyads built in the eighth century

like. We saw how simple the first mosques were. After all, Muhammad himself had said that for the believer the biggest waste of money was spending it on building. But after Muawiya the Umayyads began to think more about the fine churches they saw around them. If this was what the Christians could do, should not the Muslims put up even finer buildings to the glory of God? There was in Damascus a Christian church, built where a temple for one of the old Greek gods had stood. When the Arab armies first came there, one group had entered peacefully and another by force. They met in the middle. It was decided that the Muslims should pray in one half and the Christians should keep the other. So it went on. But Walid I wanted something grander. The Christians would not agree to sell him their half so he seized it. One Muslim, writer tells what happened:

> The Christians used to say that whoever destroyed the church would be stricken with madness and they told that to Walid. But he replied, 'I shall be the first to be stricken by madness in the service of God', and seizing an axe, he set to work to knock it down with his own hands. The Muslims on seeing that followed his example, and God

proved what the Christian had foretold to be false.

In fact he kept part of the former church, but added to it greatly and decorated it richly. The result was the building you see below. It is still called the Umayyad mosque. Who actually did the work? Walid asked the Christian emperor in Constantinople for craftsmen and we are told the emperor sent him 12,000. On your left, as you went out of the south door of the mosque – the Door of Increase, as it was called – stood the Green Palace. Here the caliphs lived. Nothing is left of it, but on page 41 you can see a picture of one of the summer palaces which the Umayyads built for themselves in the deserts outside Damascus. There they could be away from the busy city crowded round the Green Palace, and from the watching eyes of those Muslims who disapproved of rich living. They could spend their leisure time more freely.

The Umayyad mosque at Damascus

The Umayyads built in other lands as well. Below is a picture of the Dome of the Rock in the holy city of Jerusalem. Abd al-Malik began this the year after he became caliph. He meant it to be a place of prayer and pilgrimage, as Jerusalem is regarded by the Muslims as the third holy city, the others being Mecca and Medina. He also wanted to show the Christians and the Jews what Muslims could do. It is the oldest work of Muslim *architecture* still to be seen today.

The Dome of the Rock in Jerusalem

The great mosque at Kairouan

One of the most interesting mosques in the world is the Great Mosque at Kairouan. Can you pick out the minaret in this photograph? It was started in Umayyad times and is the oldest minaret still standing. The next photograph shows the mihrab and the minbar inside, put up about a hundred years after the last of the Umayyad caliphs. Can you remember from the last chapter what these are for?

LIVING UNDER THE UMAYYADS

The Muslim Arabs were only a minority in Damascus. What was it like to be a non-Muslim, say a Christian, in that part of the world in Umayyad times? Christians had to pay more tax than Muslims did. But even this was less than they were used to paying to the Byzantine emperor. To begin with, for most of the city's traders, for the scholars and students, even for the civil servants, life went on much as before. If anything, they were better off because of all the money coming into the capital from the growing Arab empire. The Arab leaders were soldiers and were glad to leave other things in their hands.

 The tax records, like other government papers, were written

Inside the great mosque

in Greek, as they had been under Byzantine rule, before the Arabs came. A great Byzantine churchman, St John of Damascus, was a top financial civil servant, until he retired to become a *monk*.

Abd al-Malik began to change things. The first wholly Islamic coins were made when he was caliph. In about the year 80/700 he changed the official language to Arabic, replacing Greek and Persian. This meant that many more people now had to learn Arabic to keep their jobs. But all through Umayyad times, most of the caliphs' advisers continued to be men of the Mediterranean – Greeks and Romans rather than Arabs. Perhaps they thought the time would come when their masters would rule the whole of this world, as the Romans had once done. Probably this is what the Umayyads wanted too.

5 *The Caliphs of Baghdad*

THE END OF THE UMAYYADS

Further east, in present-day Iraq and Persia, it was a different story.

> The Commander of the Faithful has drawn the arrows from his *quiver* and tested the wood, and found that I am the hardest. And so, by Allah, I will strip you as men strip the bark from trees. I will beat you as straying camels are beaten.

These remarks were made by a teacher's son, al-Hajjaj, whom the Ummayad caliphs had appointed governor of the lands round the Tigris and Euphrates in the days of Abd al-Malik and al-Walid. He was standing in the minbar of the mosque in Kufa, giving his opening speech to the people. Later he did a lot to start schools where there were none before. He brought water to farms by *irrigation* schemes. But no wonder he was remembered more for his cruelty in putting down rebellions, among many Arabs who still thought no Umayyad had a right to be caliph. In the end al Hajjaj died and the Umayyad family was swept from power and murdered. Just one prince escaped. He fled to distant Spain and there started a family which ruled the western part of the Arab World from Cordoba for three hundred years.

THE CITY OF BAGHDAD

In 132/750 new rulers took over at the centre of the Islamic world. They were a dynasty called in English the Abbasids, after the first member of the family to become caliph, al-Abbas.

The Eastern Gate of Baghdad which faces towards Basra

They were descended from an uncle of the prophet. What was new about them? At first they claimed they were going back to the old simple ways, with everybody having an equal place in society. This did not last. Soon they were living in just as much luxury as the Umayyads had done. But there was one big change. In 145/762 the capital was moved to Baghdad. What did this mean? The new leaders of Islam were no longer very interested in ruling the Mediterranean lands. Their eyes were more on the east – on the Tigris and Euphrates, the Gulf, the Indian Ocean and the lands that lay beyond. The advisers at their court, their secretaries and civil servants, were no longer Greeks and Syrians. They were Iraqis and Persians.

The man who actually chose the site for the new capital was al-Mansur, the second Abbasid caliph. It stood on the banks of the Tigris, only about 30 kilometres from the ruins of Ctesiphon. Not very far away are the remains of a much older capital still. Can you find out its name? And can you think why this was such a popular place for capital cities?

If you go to the top of a tall building in the centre of Baghdad today, just as it is getting dark, you see the modern city spread out below you. All is flat. In every direction, as far as you can see, are houses and more houses and twinkling lights. Hardly anything remains of al-Mansur's city, but we know quite a lot about it from the old Arab writers. It was in the shape of a circle about 2,500 metres across, and al-Mansur had the whole plan traced out on the ground before work began, so that he could get a better idea what it would look like. Around the boundary was a wall, the main part 5 metres thick, with over a hundred towers, each 20 metres high. All this was built of brick. There were four great gates. Each had the name of the place it faced towards – Kufa, Basra, Khurasan (the north-east part of Persia) and Damascus. Look at a map to find out in which direction each of them face. In the middle was an open space in which the palace and the great mosque stood. Next were the army barracks and the grand houses of the princes and the chief advisers. Then against the inside of the walls, like the spaces between the spokes of a bicycle wheel by the rim, were the housing areas for the ordinary people. But soon they were too many, and the city spread out beyond the walls and on both sides of the river. In the time of Harun al-Rashid and his son al-Mamun this was the scene of the famous stories – of the Thousand and One Arabian Nights and of Aladdin. There we can hear about life in the City of Peace, as it was called, the night adventures, the tricks and disguises, the princesses and the slave-girls, the gold and pearls, the honey cakes, the choice wine, the poor porter and the wealthy butcher, and the caliph's executioner.

Much of the city's wealth came from trade, carried on by merchants such as Sinbad the Sailor in the stories, who 'longed to roam the world in quest of profit and adventure'. A merchant would buy his stock of goods in Baghdad, anything he thought he could sell, and take them down the Tigris by river boat to Basra. There he would put to sea with fellow-merchants and a trusty crew. He might be bound for the south, to the East African coast or Zanzibar, or perhaps east to India, Sri Lanka or beyond. He would come back from all his adventures laden with what the rich wanted, pearls and precious stones, perfumes, or perhaps silks from China. He might also bring things everybody needed for cooking, peppers and spices, and also drugs for medical treatment. Wood, too, had to be imported, particularly for shipbuilding, as there was none in Persia. This would be *teak*, as well as timber from coconut palms.

This twelfth-century Arabian painting of Noah and his three sons setting out in the ark shows us what water transport was like at this time

SOME POWERFUL ABBASID CALIPHS

	AH	AD
abu-al-Abbas (al-Saffah)	132–136	750–754
al-Mansur	136–158	754–775
al-Mahdi	158–169	775–785
Harun al-Rashid	170–193	786–809
al-Mamun	198–218	813–833

Altogether there were 37 Abbasid caliphs. These are the early and famous ones. Later on the real power was in the hands of other families from other places. The caliphs just had the title. The last was killed in 656/1258.

There were many others like Sinbad, though they did not all tell such tall stories about their travels. This meant that there were always many Muslim traders on business far from home. They would not want to carry large amounts of money with them everywhere. To satisfy their needs they started something a little like our system of banks today. Some scholars think that our word 'cheque' started as an Arab word.

THE NEW LEARNING

Muslims have a saying: 'If learning were *suspended* in the farthest corners of the skies, some Persians would reach it.' Most of the Arabs who had given up the wandering life of the desert were more interested in politics and war than in studies. This was true even about studying the Arabic language. The Arabs loved to speak it and to recite and hear its poetry. But when it was a question of rules and grammar, they left that to other people like the Persians. The busy trading town Basra was also the great home of Arabic studies. Here in Harun al-Rashid's lifetime the scholar Sibawayhi wrote the most famous book on the Arabic language, so famous that people just called it Al Kitab – The Book. Producing the books themselves became easier in Abbasid times. The secret of paper-making was learnt from China. The Muslims no longer had to rely on *parchment* prepared from animal skins or expensive *papyrus* which the Egyptians made from reeds.

You probably know some people who spend a lot of time thinking about themselves. They are always talking about their own affairs and do not want to listen to new things or hear about what is going on in other countries. Such people are to be found among young and old. There are some who are quite different: they are proud of what they have done, but they don't think they are the only people who know. They are keen to learn about other things and other ways. If foreigners have made discoveries, they want to share the new knowledge. Which of these two sorts of people do you find more interesting? In Abbasid times there were many of the second sort. Islam was no longer just for the Arabs but for a growing part of the world. It was a world that looked outwards at others, not just inwards at itself. The scholars did not always concentrate on just one subject, as many do nowadays. Take Abu Rayhan Muhammad al-Biruni. He was born in 362/973 in the lands between the Caspian Sea and the Oxus. Besides being an *astronomer*, a mathematician and a student of the life sciences, he found time to master *Sanskrit*, the ancient Indian language, and so was able to write a valuable book about India. In Chapter 8 we shall have a closer look at the work of Muslim artists and scientists.

Turks arrive from the east

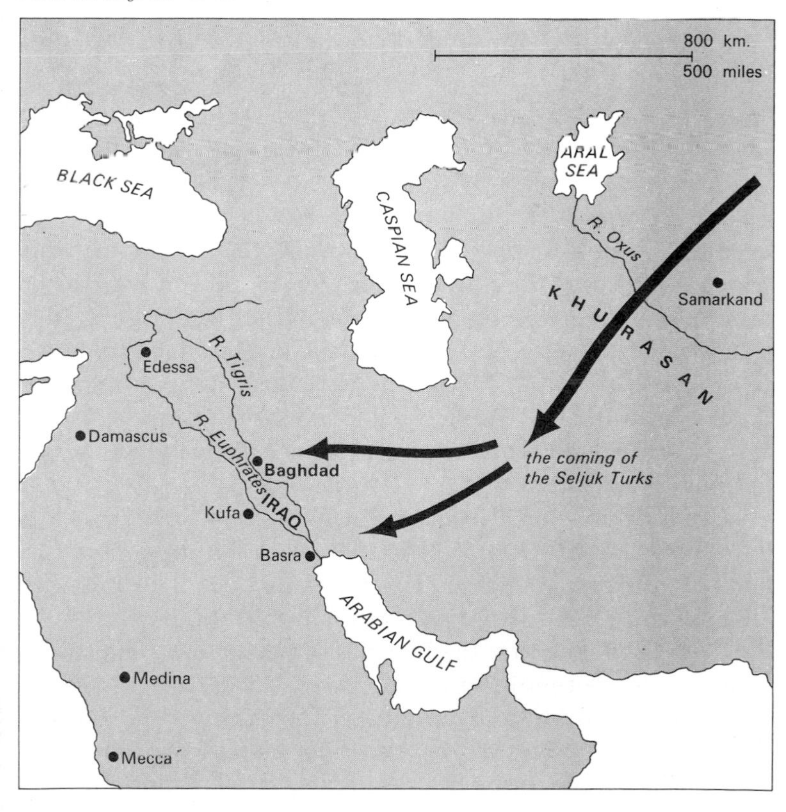

The battle for Edessa, taken from an illuminated manuscript

INVADERS FROM THE EAST

So far we have had two views of Abbasid times, the rich exciting life of Baghdad and the world of scholarly learning. There was a third: the continual struggle for power. Somewhere or another there was always fighting. The picture here shows a battle for the city of Edessa which lay on the frontiers of Byzantine and Islamic lands. The Byzantines are holding out in the tower on the left. While one force of Muslim troops attacks from outside, another has got into the city somehow and is fighting from the walls.

Here the battle was between Muslims and Christians. Often it was between Muslims and Muslims. Why should this be? One famous thinker and writer, Ibn Khaldun, put it in this way: after the time of Al-Mamun the spirit and strength of the Arabs had been weakened by the luxuries of palace life. The caliphs grew to rely more and more on other people from inside and outside the Muslim lands to protect them. But it did not stop there. 'These foreigners soon came to control the provinces', and the Abbasids were left with lands round Baghdad. Then

they even lost control of the city itself, living on there just with the title of caliph and little else.

Who were the newcomers? They were peoples from the east, from round the Caspian Sea and far beyond the Oxus. Many were Turks (but in their long move from the east they had not yet got to the country now called Turkey). We can pick out one group of Turks in particular   the Seljuks. They were named after Seljuk, their first leader. Pushing on to seek new lands, they were attracted by the Muslim way of living and became devoted believers. The buildings and works of art they left behind them are among the finest in the whole story of Islam. Their leaders wanted power and treasure as well. We are thinking of a time over 900 years ago, when the Normans far away in the west were getting ready to invade England. At about the same time, the Seljuk leaders were gradually moving in towards Baghdad. In 447/1055 they entered the city. The Abbasid caliph of that time had troubles of his own. Because the Seljuks could help him he made them welcome. After that the real power was theirs.

6 Cairo, the Fatimids and Saladin

THE FOUNDING OF THE CITY

In 1969 the people of Cairo held a festival to celebrate a thousand years of their city's life. It was founded in 358/969 on the banks of the Nile just near Fustat. This, you may remember (see page 35), was Amr's camp-town when he captured Egypt for Islam in 20/641 and became the first governor: it had been the capital ever since. So what happened in 969 to change things? How did Cairo become the Egyptian capital as it is today?

It happened like this. From Amr's time onwards the governors were always appointed by the caliphs, first the Umayyads, then the Abbasids. Most of the tax money the Egyptians paid went away to Damascus or Baghdad, where all the important decisions were made. Gradually the country got poorer and poorer. Every year the Nile brought down the rich mud with its flood waters, as it had always done, and made the land fertile. But it was no longer a land of prosperous farmers. There was one bright spot for the Egyptians, after Ibn Tulun was made governor in 254/868. He was not so interested in serving his masters in Baghdad. He saw to it that much of the tax money was kept in Egypt and that it was used to make the country richer. The noble mosque he built is named after him, and still stands. In many ways Ibn Tulun made Egypt independent. But still in his mind Islam was one state, with the caliph at Baghdad as its head. He designed his mosque as a copy of an Abbasid one in Persia.

By 969 all this was in the past. Under later governors things were almost as bad for the Egyptians as they had been before

The mosque of Ibn Tulun in Cairo

Ibn Tulun was governor. The golden age of the caliphs in Baghdad was coming to an end. But in North Africa, at Kairouan, there were new rulers. These were the Fatimid family, who claimed Muhammad's daughter Fatima, and her husband Ali, as their ancestors. These were the people who sent their armies into Egypt in 969. The Egyptians were so unhappy with Abbasid rule from Baghdad that they didn't try very hard to stop them. The Fatimids took Fustat easily. At once they gave orders to build a new city nearby. The site was chosen. Its boundaries were marked off with ropes, from which bells were hung. All the workers were ready with their hoes, waiting for the signal. The idea was that when the *astrologers* had studied the stars and decided on the best moment, the bells would be rung and the workers would begin. Sure enough a bell sounded, and the hoes began to bite into the ground. But it was too soon. A bird had perched on one of the ropes and started the ringing. The astrologers were shocked. They believed it was quite the wrong time to start: the planet al-Qahira or Mars, had risen over the eastern horizon. What could be done? They thought the only way to keep bad luck from the city was to give it the planet's name. So they called it Al-Qahira. As the years passed, this became in English, Cairo.

THE FATIMIDS

This was how in 969 the Fatimids arrived in Egypt, and began their two hundred years of rule from Cairo. One thing that made them strong to begin with was their army.

The Fatimids did not just want to rule North Africa and be independent of the Abbasids and Baghdad. Can you think back to the first sad division in the Muslim world, between Shiites (followers of the family of Fatima and Ali) on one side, and the rest (the Sunnis) on the other? The Abbasid caliphs

An ink drawing of two Fatimid soldiers

Al-Azhar mosque

were Sunnis. From what you have read about them, what do you think the Fatimids were? They too called themselves caliphs – leaders who came after the prophet. They did not think the Abbasids had any right to be called caliphs at all. They saw themselves as leaders of the whole Muslim world. They never succeeded in spite of all their efforts. Instead, they split the Muslims. They are remembered now for what they did as rulers of Egypt. They are also remembered for the tradition of learning which they founded.

The picture above shows part of al-Azhar mosque as it looks today, though it was much smaller and simpler then. It was the first the Fatimids built in Cairo. They meant it not only for prayers and the Friday assembly, but also as a college to train people to spread Shiite ideas throughout Islam. When Fatimid rule ended it came into the hands of the Sunnis. After some time it became a place of learning once more, so famous that students flocked to it from all over the Islamic world. In the words of a modern Egyptian writer: 'In spite of differences of nationality and race, they gathered here under one roof, and Al-Azhar became a second Kaba to which people made pilgrimage throughout the whole year.' Today, as Al-Azhar

University, it has over 150 thousand students. Apart from all its printed books, the library has a collection of fifteen thousand *manuscripts*. It is the home of the Quran box in the picture on page 25.

THE COMING OF SALADIN

The first three Fatimid caliphs were powerful men who ruled personally. Later Fatimids had the same sort of problems as the Abbasids did in Baghdad. Most were more interested in a life of pleasure and rich living than in governing and protecting their lands. None of them was able to control the generals,

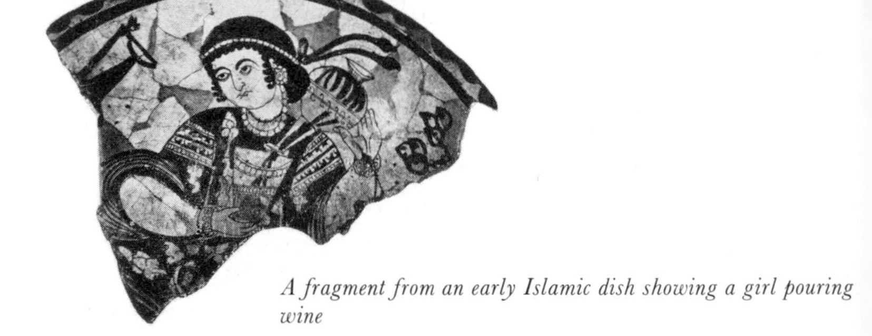

A fragment from an early Islamic dish showing a girl pouring wine

who became the real rulers in one takeover after another. There was trouble from outside as well. We are coming to the time of the wars that Europeans call the *crusades* – the wars of the Christian cross. This was when the kings in western Europe tried to take back from the Muslims Jerusalem and the lands where Christianity began. There is another Then and There book, 'The Crusades', about these happenings.

On the side of Islam the most famous man was Salah al-Din al-Ayyubi. We know him in English as Saladin, the general who united the Muslims in Syria and Egypt to drive out the invaders. What sort of a man was he? He came from the hilly lands north of Iraq and Syria. As a boy he lived with his father in Damascus. Most of the men in his family were soldiers.

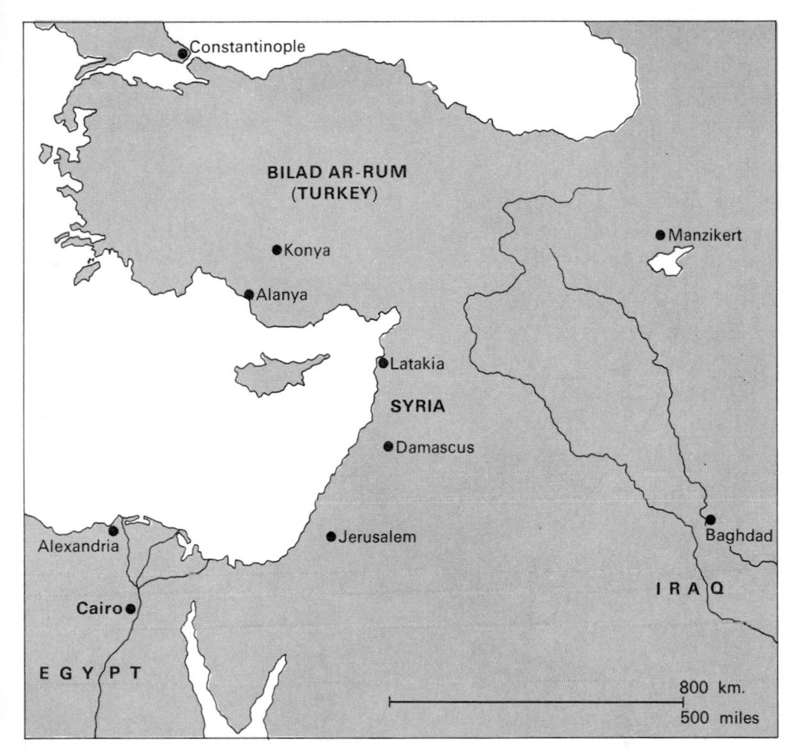

The Middle East at the time of Saladin and after

Everyone who has read about the crusades knows how the Christians respected him as an honourable man and a brave and fair fighter. As a Muslim he was a Sunni, and as such he was no lover of the Fatimids. When his uncle led an army to Egypt to guard against a crusader attack, Saladin went too. Then his uncle died and that gave him his chance. At once he made himself master of Egypt. Nobody stood in his way. Soon afterwards, in 567/1171, the Fatimid caliph also died, and Saladin saw to it that nobody took over from him. That was the end of Shiite rule. The next rulers of Egypt were called sultans: they did not claim they were caliphs of the whole Muslim world.

Cairo was Saladin's capital, from which he ruled Egypt and Syria until his death in 589/1193. What is there now to remind us of him? Above the city stand the Mukattam Hills.

From the top you can look out over the Nile and Cairo itself, and in the distance you can even see the *pyramids*. It is a wonderful sight. Here Saladin decided to build his headquarters, known today as the *Citadel*. He planned towers and a strong wall, with mosques and palaces inside it. Building soon began, but he did not live to see it all finished. The work was carried on by the sultans who followed him – called the Ayyubids, after his father.

Part of the Cairo Citadel showing one of the gateways

We have seen governors, caliphs and sultans come and go. Each family, or dynasty, has given its name to the times in which it lived. You can see them set out in the chart on page 92. But for many Egyptians life went on from year to year, no matter who was in power in the palaces. From the time of the first Fatimids they were building up their own Egyptian way of life within the wider world of Islam. Then and under later rulers Cairo came more and more to take the place of Baghdad as the greatest trading city, the magnet for scholars, artists and craftsmen. It even became the main centre for religious studies. One traveller, called Ibn Battuta, about whom you can read more in Chapter 9, called it

> mother of cities, mistress of broad regions and fruitful lands, boundless in the number of its buildings, without equal in beauty and splendour, the meeting-place of comer and goer, the halting-place of the feeble and the mighty, whose crowds surge as the waves of the sea and can scarcely be contained in her for all her size and capacity.

Above left: *A fourteenth-century Egyptian drawing of three prisoners*

Above: *An early Islamic candlestick made in Egypt*

Left: *A fourteenth-century Egyptian glass vase with enamelled decoration*

7 *Living in Towns*

THE ARAB HOUSE

Think about your own house. What is your problem? Keeping warm or keeping cool? Perhaps both, at different times of the year. On the whole, people who live in Britain think more about being warm in the winter and keeping out cold air. At the same time they like to have plenty of windows facing outwards to let in what light there is, particularly in the winter. The sun is a friend.

Any house built with this in mind would be quite wrong for the people we have been reading about. In the hot dry Arab lands you need something different. There are two problems: how to shelter from the burning heat of the day, and how to make the best use of the cool air at night. What was the answer? What were houses like in the great cities and towns in the central lands of Islam?

The first point is that these town houses did not face outwards on to the street. Outside there was all the glaring heat, and the city dust and noise. Instead the idea was to make each house a little world on its own, calm and cool. In the centre was the *sahn* – the courtyard. It was open to the sky and planted with trees. Round it were the living areas: one side of each of these rooms had no wall and was open towards the sahn. At night the colder air passed into these rooms round the sahn, and remained to keep the house cool for much of the day. By day you could sit round the sahn in the shade and look up at the sky above you. When it got really hot you could go further back into the *iwan*, or recess, where the deepest shade was. The picture here is of an old house of this kind in Cairo, but you could find the

The courtyard of a house in Cairo

same thing all over the Arab world.

Even the sight of water refreshes you in the heat. To people used to the desert, it would be a special pleasure to see the running water in fountains and pools. That is why to this day water is so important in gardens and public places in the Arab lands. And that is why it is counted as one of the rewards of the faithful in paradise after death. As the Quran says: 'Those that believe in Allah and do what is right shall be forgiven their sins and admitted to gardens watered by running streams, where they shall dwell for ever.' So in this life the house should have its water. Usually there was a basin in the middle of the sahn with a fountain playing in it. If there was not enough water for that, you could have water trickling into the basin over a flat piece of marble. This is called a *salsabil*. The surface is carved with a pattern to give the idea of a running stream with the surface ruffled by the breeze.

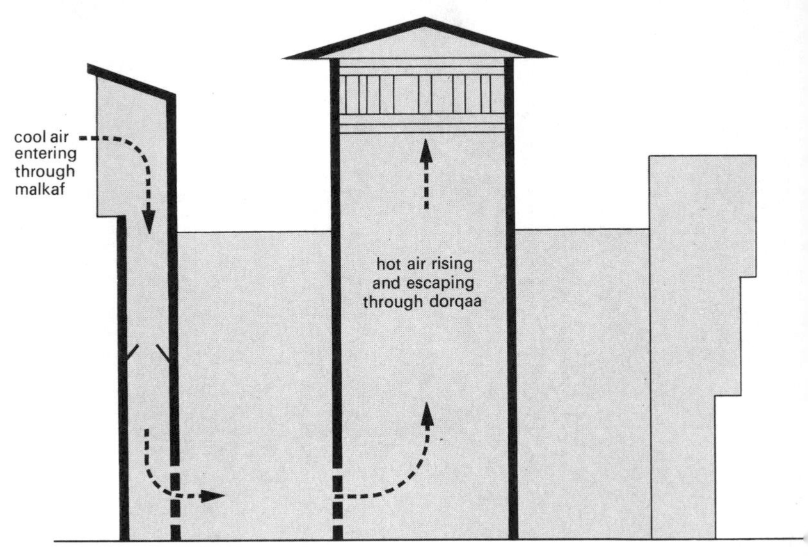

A malkaf cooling system

As time went on, there was another development in designing houses. Builders discovered how to roof over the courtyard without losing the coolness of the sahn system. This meant making a sort of covered courtyard called a *dorqaa*. Its roof is much higher than the roof of the building and there are spaces through which the hot air can get out as it rises from the house. What takes its place? Above the house too is a shaft, left open near the top on the side the cool breeze comes from. So when the hot air rises to the top of the dorqaa and out, fresh air is drawn down the shaft to replace it. This shaft is called a *malkaf*. The diagram above shows how the malkaf system works.

Another way of letting air pass freely without letting in the glare of the sun is the *mushrabeya*. You can see one on the next page. The grill with its pattern breaks up the light but does not stop the air. Of course this is just the opposite of what a glass window pane does.

A mushrabeya

AT THE CENTRE OF THE CITY

Once outside the peace and coolness of the house you were right in the bustling city. We saw how in the early years of Islam the mosques were the centres of Muslim city life. So they remained. Next to them you could usually find the *bazaars* and the main business houses. People in the same sort of business stuck together. So, in Damascus in later times, all the coppersmiths had their stores and workshops on the south side of the Umayyad mosque, reached through the Door of Increase where the Green Palace of the Umayyads had once stood. If you left the mosque by the east side you went through the Door of the Hours, the largest of all. Why did it have this name? Just by it was a huge 'clock' worked by water-power. There were little wooden doors to mark the hours, green inside and yellow outside. As each hour passed, another door was turned to show its green face. The Door of the Hours led to the cloth merchants' shops. Above them were the jewellers, the booksellers and the glassmakers. Here, too, you could buy pens, paper and ink from the stationers. To visit the candlemakers or the fruitsellers you went through the west

A cluster of old houses in Damascus

door, the Door of the Post. The northern one was called the Door of the *Confectioners*.

Water was important in these public places, just as in people's houses. By each of the four doors was a building with about a hundred rooms in it, for washing before prayer. Near the Door of the Confectioners stood a large lavatory, supplied with running water. Then there were the public baths. As in Greek and Roman cities, these were for meeting your friends and spending some of your spare time just as much as for having a bath. One visitor to Baghdad thought the arrangements in the baths were splendid; 'Every bather is given three towels, one to wear round his waist when he goes in, another to wear round his waist when he comes out, and the third to dry himself with.'

You could expect to find all this, or something like it, at the centre of many of the cities of Islam. Nearby also stood the palace of the ruler: the caliph or sultan, or the governor appointed by him. Here would be the barracks for his guards.

Close to these you might find special places where foreigners lived, or people of other religions, such as Jews.

Around the centre were the houses of the townspeople. To a stranger it might seem just a tangle of hot dusty streets and alleys: but, as we know, the houses were built to live in and not to look at from outside. Then as you got further out from the centre the buildings became fewer. You might well see the rough huts put up by people who had nothing else to shelter them, or perhaps by newcomers from the countryside.

The outside of old city houses in Saudi Arabia

LIVING TOGETHER

If you live in a town, you know how neighbours rely on each other when there is trouble. If you are ill or need help from outside, you probably know where to go and who to see: it may be the doctor, or you may have to find somebody in a government office or the town hall. In the cities we have been talking about, things very much depended on the ruler himself. There was a governor in Harun al-Rashid's time called Tahir ibn al Hussein. He gave his son some advice about what a good ruler should do. 'Tax everybody,' he wrote, 'in a fair and just manner.' Nobody should be let off paying tax, 'not even your own officials or *courtiers* or followers.' Nobody was to be charged tax he hadn't enough money to pay. What should the ruler do with his money? It was no good hoarding it or locking it up in a safe. Then what was the answer?

> Take care of the poor, the widows and the orphans; pay them special pensions from your treasury. Do the same to the blind and to those who can recite the Quran. And, provided this does not overburden the treasury, build hospitals for sick Muslims, with a staff of physicians and attendants who will cure them and look after their needs.

Apart from the ruler and his taxes, there were others who could help. Many rich people remembered the third Pillar of Islam and left money to be used for *charity* after they died. In Damascus these charities were so many, that nobody could count them. Some gave money to make pavements in the city lanes and keep them in repair. There were charities to help with expenses for travellers, particularly pilgrims. Others provided wedding outfits for brides whose families couldn't afford them. But here is a more surprising one, as a visitor from north Africa described it. 'One day as I went along a lane in Damascus I saw a small slave who had dropped a Chinese *porcelain* dish, which was broken to bits.' People gathered round and somebody advised him to take the pieces to the person who looked after the charity for pots and dishes. He did so, and was given enough money to buy another one like it. 'This *benefaction* is indeed a mender of hearts – may God richly reward him whose zeal for good works rose to such heights!'

8 *Artists and Scientists*

THE USES OF WRITING

Why do we write? For others to read. And what better reading could a Muslim have than the Quran itself? So how better could you spend your life than by making copies of the Quran? Those who had the gift of doing so were greatly honoured by their fellow Muslims. They were sure of a reward in the next life. In this life, writing beautifully – the art of *calligraphy* – was valued more than any other art in the great cities we have read about. One such calligrapher was Ali ibn Ibrahim al-Hafiz, who in 1328 finished his sixty-ninth copy of the Quran. In this copy he noted down how many he had already finished. He also wrote that his life ambition was to make a hundred or more copies, God willing.

When people were always on the move, there was not much chance for them to practise a fine style of handwriting. As one Arab historian put it: 'When the Companions of the Prophet began to write out the letters of the Quran, their handwriting being somewhat shaky, many of the letters they drew differed from the shapes accepted by the calligraphers.' So over the years a number of different ways of writing Arabic developed. You can see some of these in the chart on page 70 There are two main styles to think of. First Kufic, named after the city of Kufa where it was much used. You can tell the various kinds of Kufic script because there are always sharp points in the letters. The top three examples in the chart are all Kufic. The second main style is Nakshi. Here we have no sharp points, but smooth curves instead. The last three examples are all of this style. The last of all is in a script called

Arabic writing styles

Nastaliq: it is much used today, and was invented about 600 years ago by Mir Ali Tabrizi. You might like to look at the photographs of pages from the Quran in Chapter 2 and see which style each of them comes closest to.

Calligraphers, like other Muslim artists, were very interested in shapes and patterns. They found the Arabic letters themselves very convenient to use in this way. Look at the drawing of the Fatimid soldiers on page 56. Can you pick out the Kufic inscription above their heads? In drawing this, the artist was giving people the message 'Glory and good fortune to the leader Abu Mansur'. But more than that, he made it good to look at. Without reading Arabic we can enjoy the pattern as part of the whole work.

PATTERNS AND BUILDINGS

Other ideas came from watching how plants grow, with

curving stem and the leaves and flowers unfolding to the same pattern, one after another. Here is a picture of a bowl in which the potter has used both letters and flowers in his design. Such patterns were worked out not just for small things like this, but for the whole surface of a building. You can see many examples in any book about the art of Islam which has pictures in colour.

A sixteenth-century Turkish bowl

Architects could also use the shapes of the actual materials they were building with as you can see from the pictures on the next two pages. The first is a brick tower made nearly a thousand years ago in Konya. From the photograph you can see some of the designs the architect worked out, just using the shape of the bricks. He could first draw patterns by geometry, like the ones in the second picture, and base his designs on them. The third picture shows something else. In this case he has designed the bricks to be laid at different depths in the wall, so as to make raised patterns with them. As the direction of the sunlight changes during the day, so the shadows from the raised bricks will move. And as the shadows move, a new set of patterns will always be growing before your eyes.

A Turkish tower showing the patterns the builders made with bricks

Patterns drawn using geometry

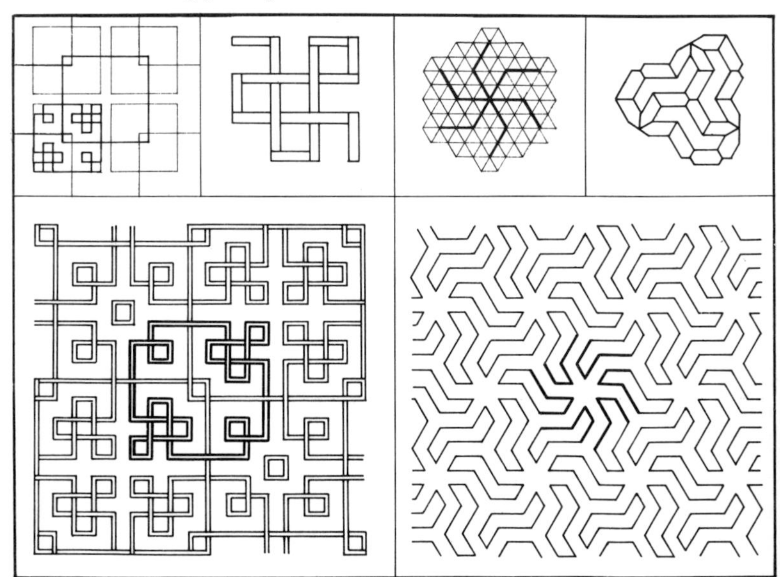

Raised brickwork

A SIGN FOR ZERO

We noticed before how keen Muslim thinkers were to learn from what others outside Islam had discovered. When the Arab armies burst out of Arabia and Islam spread, the learning of the Greek philosophers and scientists in the Byzantine lands, that of the Persians, and of the Hindus in India – all were open to them. The Prophet was clear about the duty of Muslims in this situation: 'Seek knowledge, in China if necessary.'

Much of the most advanced scientific work in the world at that time had been done by the Greeks. But one thing had held them back: they only had a very clumsy way of writing numerals, using letters of the alphabet, and they could not express fractions in a convenient way. These are the Roman numerals up to ten:

I II III IV V VI VII VIII IX X

You can tell how little help they would be to anybody trying to do written sums. Apart from the difficulty of writing down and comparing particular numbers, there was an even greater one. Have you ever tried to work out a calculation without any sign for zero? For instance try to add up quickly:

XXIX
XLI
LX

Neither the Greeks nor the Romans had a zero sign.

What all these peoples had in common was that they counted in tens. In India, Hindu mathematicians had already started using a special sign for writing each number from 1 to 9. They then hit on the idea of using a separate sign for zero – the 0 we all know. So the sum above in Roman numerals becomes:

29
41
60

How simple it seems, but what a great step forward for human knowledge! Muslim mathematicians were quick to start using these numerals. Europeans then learnt from them, which is why, in English, we call them 'Arabic numerals.' Algebra, which is really the Arabic al-jabr, is something else which came to Europe from the world of Islam. (The word means making good what is broken, filling in something which is incomplete.) Like Muslim scholars in other studies, the Muslim mathematicians did not just copy other people.

TRAVELLERS AND MAPMAKERS

One of our great needs is to be able to measure accurately. Here the scientists of Islam made great progress in the times we have been reading about. Religion encouraged them, particularly the astronomers. Each day and night you needed to know exactly the five times for prayer. Again, you had to know the direction of Mecca for your own prayer, and architects had to place the mihrab rightly in a mosque. Measuring these successfully meant you had to observe where the sun, the moon and the stars were in relation to our earth. Opposite are examples of the instruments which were developed and used in the Islamic world to help in this.

The same sort of instruments and the same sort of skills

Early Muslim navigational instruments:

Left: *Part of a fourteenth-century ivory sundial*

Below: *A miniature Persian sundial*

Below left: *A thirteenth-century Egyptian astrolabe*

were sometimes needed in finding your way. For long journeys across the desert you needed to know the right direction, and where you were, just as much as a sailor would at sea. In fact the first Muslim *navigators* worked on land. Navigating ships came later, when the caliphs and the sultans spread their

A copy of one of the maps made for Roger of Sicily by Al-Idrisi

power across the Mediterranean and the Indian Ocean. The instruments of those days were not accurate enough to give all the answers needed. In *navigation* there were still many problems to solve. But in Islam more was known about them than in western Europe.

There was a Norman king, Roger of Sicily, who wanted the best information about geography. This was in about 1150. He turned to the Arab mapmaker Al-Idrisi, who made him a plan of the world, as far as it was then known, in silver. Al-Idrisi was one of the scholars who had learnt from the geographers of the ancient Greek world: he added his own studies and also used the Arabic books of charts and sailing instructions of his own times. To go with the silver plan he drew seventy-one maps and wrote a book of world geography. The maps have now disappeared, but above is a copy of one of them, made much later.

THE DOCTORS

 In the Middle Ages there was a very popular ointment you

could buy in France. It was supposed to cure almost anything, which of course it did not. It was called Blanc de Razes, after a very famous Arab doctor and scholar Al-Razi. The interesting thing is not the ointment itself, but its name. The shopkeepers knew that with Al-Razi's name people would buy it. This is just one of the things that show how western Europeans trusted the medical knowledge of the Muslim world.

Abu Bakr al-Razi came from near Teheran in Persia, and died in 313/925. Before his lifetime, and indeed before Islam, another Persian town had become the world's leading medical centre. This was Gondeshapur, near Hira. Here came Jews and Christians, Greeks and Syrians, Persians and Hindus, as students and teachers. And so it continued under the Abbasid caliphs. Al-Mamun had the books of the Greek medical scientists translated into Arabic. Soon new medical textbooks based on these were being used all over Islam.

Al-Razi was not happy just to accept what other authorities said. He kept a careful record, like a diary, of all the patients he treated, setting down their symptoms and how they changed, what he did, and what were the results. From all this he could draw his conclusions. You may have had measles yourself, or you will know somebody who has. It is very unlikely that you will have had smallpox – something much more serious: this is because, through vaccination, smallpox has been stamped out nearly everywhere. Al-Razi wrote the earliest book we have about infectious diseases, in which he set out clearly the difference between measles and smallpox. Vaccination was not discovered till hundreds of years later, but he had taken the first step – gathering the real facts about the disease. Two other books of his, translated into Latin, became the main ones for medical students in western Europe in the Middle Ages.

At the end of the last chapter we saw how money was given for building hospitals and running them. The larger hospitals in the great cities were teaching centres as well. For the patients, each hospital had separate sides for men and women. The hospital director was helped by specialists in charge of the different departments and wards, with their own staffs of

A thirteenth-century pharmacy in which medicine is being prepared from honey

nurses and other workers. The head *pharmacist* ran the *pharmacy* where medicines were made up according to the doctors' orders. Here you see the scene in one pharmacy, painted in Baghdad in 681/1224.

Now we have had a glimpse at the work of artists and scientists in the world of Islam. Perhaps you will want to find out more. Meanwhile here is one thing to think about. Do you remember Al-Biruni, another scholar of Abbasid times, whom we read about in Chapter 5? He wrote a life of Al-Razi and made a list of his books. Altogether Al-Razi had written 175. Besides his medical works and the books on mathematics and philosophy, he experimented and wrote on chemistry and many other sciences. Al-Biruni himself was still working on a book of *pharmacology* when he was eighty, and studied even more widely than Al-Razi.

Both of them had one thing in common. They were not satisfied with one small branch of knowledge. So far as could be done in those times, they wanted to explore the whole tree.

9 *One Man's Journeys*

MONGOLS AND MAMLUKS

By the time we are talking about, the Abbasids, the Fatimids, Saladin and his family – all had gone. Cairo and Damascus were still rich and busy cities, particularly Cairo. But as for Baghdad, most of the old city was in ruins: what was left was little more than a village. What had happened? A Muslim writer at the time called it the worst disaster in all history. In about 600/1200 a certain Temujin (the name means 'smith') was trying to make himself lord of the Mongol peoples far away in eastern Asia. He succeeded, and they gave him the title Chingis Khan. Under him the terrible Mongol armies, mounted on their swift horses, crushed everybody in their way. He conquered China, he conquered Russia., His soldiers swept down on the Muslim lands, killing and wrecking, then riding on. After Chingis Khan's death, his grandson Hulegu in 656/1258 took Baghdad, and had the last Abbasid caliph killed. Two years after that, in 658/1260, he took Damascus as well. It seemed there was nothing to stop him reaching Egypt, or even Arabia and Mecca itself. But later that year, in the month of Ramadan, his armies were beaten for the first time.

This was the work of the new rulers of Egypt. Saladin's family had been followed by new sultans, the Mamluks. So it was the Mamluk army that turned back the Mongols and saved Islam. The Mongols never got any further, and by the middle of the eighteenth century, the Mamluk sultans were the greatest power in western Islam, ruling all Egypt and Syria. East of that the Mongols were still the masters. But the Mongol rulers of Iraq and Persia had become Muslims themselves.

Muslim scholars and Muslim artists were at work again.

THE TRAVELLER OF ISLAM

A half a century after the first defeat of the Mongols by the Mamluk army, a man was born who was to become very well-known for his travels and adventures in the Muslim world. His name was Ibn Battuta.

Somebody has worked out that he travelled 75,000 miles, (120,000 kilometres) on foot, by camel and on horseback. He visited every part of the Muslim world. He made the pilgrimage to Mecca seven times. While in India he fell into the hands of bandits and just managed to get away with his life: twice he was nearly captured by pirates in the Mediterranean. He went all the way to Peking. No wonder he was known as 'the traveller of Islam'. For his time (before modern transport) he could be called the travel champion of the world.

Ibn Battuta was born in Tangier, in Morocco, in 703/1304. When he was twenty-one he started out on his first pilgrimage. His last great journey nearly thirty years later, took him across the Sahara to the lands of the Niger. When he came back home for the last time, he told his story at the court of the sultan of Morocco. Everybody was amazed. Many of his listeners refused to believe him. What he had to say was far outside anything people knew about other countries in those days. But the sultan himself was so impressed that he instructed one of his chief secretaries to write out the complete account of Ibn Battuta's adventures as he dictated it.

So far we have watched the growing Muslim world as it split up into different states. We have seen the rulers go their separate ways and even fight each other. But all this time one thing united Muslims from every land in a wonderful way, as it does now: the need to visit Mecca once in your lifetime if you possibly can. Ibn Battuta's book tells us better than anything else what it was like to be in the Islamic world in the time Europeans call the Middle Ages. We cannot go with him everywhere, but through his eyes we can look again at the ancient lands of Islam. We can go to some of the places far from the rule of the caliphs where more and more people were beginning to turn to the Muslim way of life.

To Ibn Battuta, as a north African, Egypt was the leader of Islam. Cairo was the first great city he saw on his travels. He left home in 725/1325 'with the intention of making the Pilgrimage to the Holy House and the Tomb of the Prophet'. Even the first part of his journey was not an easy one. Twice on the way from Tangier he got fever and at one point he had to tie himself in the saddle with a turban-cloth 'in case I should fall by reason of my weakness'. It took him nearly a year to reach Cairo. It was his description of the city that we read at the end of Chapter 6.

The Mamluks ruled as soldiers and in some ways their rule was hard and cruel. But for many Egyptians they brought happiness and more prosperous times. Many traders with India and the east earned riches for the country. Ibn Battuta does not tell us a great deal about how he spent his time in Cairo. But he would certainly have visited Al-Azhar university and so would have seen the Quran box on page 25 in the library there. In the mosques he would have seen many richly decorated glass lamps, Egyptians were particularly good at glass-making. A lamp was usually bought as an offering, perhaps by a wealthy businessman. On page 61 is a candlestick offered by one of the Mamluk sultans.

In Egypt Ibn Battuta first began to think of going farther afield. One day the man he was staying with told him: 'I see that you are fond of travelling through foreign lands.' Ibn Battuta had not really thought this out but he said, 'Yes, I am.' His host went on, 'You must certainly visit my brother Farid in India, and my brother Rukn in Sind, and my brother Burhan in China, and when you find them give them greeting from me.' Ibn Battuta was amazed. But now the idea was in his mind, and in the end he did go on travelling until he had met all three and given them the greeting as he was told.

But all this was far in the future. Ibn Battuta could not take the usual way from Cairo to Mecca, up the Nile valley and across the Red Sea, as there was fighting along the route. So he spent a few weeks visiting Jerusalem and the cities of Syria, finishing up at Damascus. It was Ramadan – the ninth month, the fasting month. He stayed until the festival Id al-Fitr, which marks the end of the fast. Then at once he joined the great pilgrim caravan which set out each year from Damascus across Syria and the deserts, to reach Mecca in time for the performance of the Hajj in the last month of the year. 'Thus,' he said, 'we reached the goal of our hopes, the City of *Surety*, Mecca (may God ennoble her!), where we immediately entered the holy *sanctuary* and began the *rites* of pilgrimage.'

He had no sooner made this first pilgrimage than he was planning to come back next year for his second. He filled the months between by seeing as many as he could of the cities of Iraq. Then he returned to Mecca along the most famous pilgrim route of all, from Baghdad to Mecca. Long before, the wife of the caliph Harun al-Rashid had used her fortune to have *cisterns* built where water could be stored at resting places on the route. This time he stayed in Mecca for three years. Why so long? He was determined to go on with his religious studies and learn all he could about Muslim law. Mecca was the place where the best teachers were. With this training he was sure of a special welcome wherever he went. More than that, it often meant he could be made a *qadi*, or judge, in the places he visited. In those days Muslim countries still shared the same laws.

A VISIT TO TURKEY

At one point Ibn Battuta decided to visit 'the country of the Turks' – today's Turkey. Most people then called it Bilad-ar-Rum, the Land of the Romans; earlier it had all been part of the Roman and then the Byzantine empires. The Turks we are talking of were the Seljuk Turks we have met before – the people from the east who had overrun the Abbasid lands and taken Baghdad. Some of them had pressed on into the Byzantine lands and defeated the Byzantine emperor in a great battle at Manzikert in 463/1071. This group became known as the Seijuks of Rum, and soon they were ruling most of

The dockyard at Alanya

present-day Turkey except for small areas round Constantinople.

Ibn Battuta was lucky enough to get a free passage in a Christian ship and ten days' sailing from Latakis on the Syrian coast brought him to Alanya. On his left as they drew into the little harbour were the dockyards, just as you would see them today. They had been made a hundred years before for shipbuilding by one of the great Seljuk sultans, Ala al-Din Kay-Qubad. This is a fertile coast, where the land along the Mediterranean is sheltered from the cold north by the Taurus mountains, snow-covered in winter. Today it is known for its delicious fruits; in Ibn Battuta's time it was also one of the places from which Egypt got timber. But, above all, Ibn Battuta found the people kinder than any he had ever met. In one place they almost came to blows deciding who should be the ones to entertain him. All over the Muslim world along the main caravan routes were places for pilgrims or any other travellers to stay. They stood a day's journey apart, about 30 kilometres. Food and lodging were usually free, provided by the ruler or the ordinary people. None were more splendid than the *hans* (as these places were called) built by the Seljuks of Rum. The old Seljuk capital was Konya, then, as now, a city of wide streets, many streams and fruit gardens. Ibn Battuta spent some days there as guest of the local qadi. Such a man would be very glad of his company as a scholar and theologian. At Konya too he could visit the important college for teaching religion which was in a fine building.

AFRICAN KINGDOMS

Another of Ibn Battuta's journeys took him far to the south. Here was Zanzibar, as early Arab travellers called that island. The name means 'the coast of the Zanj', that is 'of the Africans'. But what Ibn Battuta really wanted to see was the great city of Kilwa, a little further south. About this time its people were building a noble mosque. On a cliff a hundred feet above the sea was Husuni Kubwa, the sultan's palace. It was built with blocks of coral and had more than a hundred rooms. The sultan at the time of Ibn Battuta's visit had a great name for being a generous giver. Ibn Battuta wrote: 'I have seen him give the clothes off his back to a beggar who asked him for them.' While in Kilwa, Ibn Battuta heard stories of Sofala – a fortnight's journey still further south – where the merchants bought gold from central Africa in exchange for porcelain from China and glass from India and Europe. His book is just one of the ways we know about the cities of the east African coast, like Kilwa in Tanzania and Mombasa in Kenya, which were busy and thriving long before any Europeans went there.

Ibn Battuta's last great journey was over twenty years later, in 753/1352. How old do you think he was then? By that time the only region of Islam he had not visited was the kingdom of Mali, which lay across the Sahara desert. People were still talking about the hajj of the famous Mansa Musa, who had died some years before. Mansa means sultan or king, and Mansa Musa had made Mali one of the largest empires in the world. He had left his capital for Cairo and Mecca with nearly a hundred camels loaded with gold – gifts for charity and for those who helped him on his way. In Mecca he had met a Spanish poet and architect called as-Sahili, who agreed to go back with him to Mali. As-Sahili was the man who designed the oldest west African mosques that survive today. You can see the kind of mosque from the picture opposite.

A mosque in Timbuktu in the style of as-Sahili

A man from Spain, met on the sacred pilgrimage, living in Mali: this again shows how Islam was not for one place or one race, but for the world.

Now back to Ibn Battuta's journey. The real starting point was Sijilmasa, where he bought camels and four months' food for them. Then he set off with a merchant caravan. The journey across the Sahara to Walata, the southern terminus, took them exactly two months. Once they lost one of the party: in the end he must have died of thirst. The most dangerous stage was the last.

> From this point the *takshif* is sent out. The takshif is a man who is hired by the people in the caravan to go ahead to Walata, carrying letters from them to their friends there.

> Their friends then come out a distance of four nights' journey to meet the caravan, and bring water with them. It often happens that the takshif dies in the desert, so that the people of Walata know nothing about the caravan, and all or most of those who are with it die. There is no visible road or track in these parts – nothing but sand blown hither and thither by the wind. I noticed, as a strange thing, that the guide whom we had was blind in one eye, and diseased in the other, yet he had the best knowledge of the road of any man.

All was well, and one night 'we saw with joy the fires of the party who had come out to meet us'. From there on there was no need to go in a caravan and three weeks later Ibn Battuta was in the city of Mali.

Mansa Musa and the other mansas were black African rulers. As you can see from the map, their chief towns lay along the river Niger whose water kept them alive. The city of Mali itself in those days spread out over several square kilometres, and was nearly surrounded by various branches of the Niger. In the centre were the great markets, full of goods from Cairo and north Africa, metalwork and rich cloth of silk and wool, as well as all the local produce. As you got further out from the city centre you would find many more houses standing among farms. There was plenty of grain, millet in particular. There were sheep and cattle for food – and for leather. It is good land for cotton too. From December for about five months the ground was almost as bare as the desert: but by September, around harvest time, you could walk between the ripening crops of grain so high that you could hardly see the thatched round roofs of the houses. The gold Mansa Musa used came from river beds further south: trade in this was what made Mali rich.

What about the people Ibn Battuta met? Mansa Musa had died and his brother was mansa instead. Ibn Battuta did not think much of him – but this was just because he did not give him large presents as Mansa Musa would have done. There

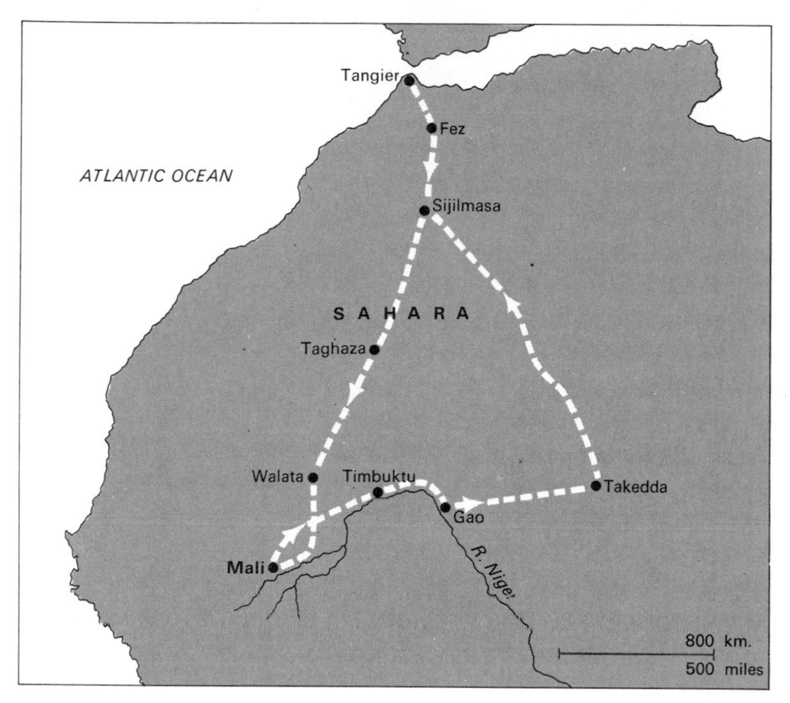

Ibn Battuta's last journey. As the arrows show, he started off from Tangier, crossed the Sahara desert and made his way back by a different route

were some Mali customs he did not like either. What really made him happy was the way people kept the hours of prayer and brought up their children in the Muslim faith. If you did not go to the mosque early on Fridays, you could not find a corner left to pray in, because of the crowds. You always put on clean clothes that day. In Mali, Ibn Battuta says: 'Even if a man has nothing but an old worn shirt, he washes it and cleans it, and wears it to the Friday service.' Above all, he tells how Malians loved justice. 'There is complete security in their country. Neither traveller nor *inhabitant* in it has anything to fear from robbers or men of violence.'

At last it was time to move on. But before turning for home, Ibn Battuta rode to Timbuktu, then took a boat down the Niger to Gao. Finally he joined a big merchant caravan and made his way back to his own city.

10 Then and Now

With the story of Ibn Battuta and his world this book ends. We have read about Muhammad's life. We have seen what it was like to live when the Muslims were taking new lands and winning over more and more people to share their faith and their beliefs. And this was not all. As people from other societies joined them, there was a sharing and mixing of ideas across the countries and continents. Beliefs about God and his Prophet did not change: but round them Muslims built a new way of life. This was the world of Islam. This is what this book has been about.

Then what happened? Things began to go badly for the Muslims. The crusades had taught them to look on the Europeans in the west as enemies. Then from the east came Chingis Khan, who put an end to the life of old Baghdad. Later still, a few years after Ibn Battuta's death, there was another much more brutal invader from the east, Timur the Lame – Tamerlane as he is called in English. As all these troubles hit them they gradually stopped looking out at other societies. They began to feel that everything outside Islam must be bad, and that there was nothing to be gained from mixing with non-believers. Within Islam itself the idea grew that all there was to know had already been written down: you only had to read it, and then there was nothing else to learn or discover.

Thinking like this, people became afraid to change old things or to face new things. The history of books is a good example. The Muslims had discovered the secret of making paper in 751 when they had fought a battle with the Chinese and had taken prisoner some men who were skilled in paper-making. The Muslims had made use of this skill and were far ahead of the Europeans at this time. Then in the 1400s, not so very long after Tamerlane, men in western Europe began to use paper and also discovered the art of printing. This meant that hundreds of books could be produced from the same blocks of type, instead of having to write each copy separately by hand. Many more people had the chance to read and learn. You might think Muslims would have welcomed this discovery too. But in fact they refused to have anything to do with it for nearly three hundred years.

By then, well into the 1700s, what we call the industrial revolution had started in Europe. In technical matters the western countries were far ahead. The Muslims could only watch them getting richer and growing in political power. Many now began to copy western styles and western habits without thinking which were suitable and which were not. Often old ways of doing things were thrown aside just because they were not western.

So which were right? Those who would not allow the new, or those who wanted to sweep away everything old? Those who thought printing was against their religion, or those who thought that European hats must always be better than Arab *turbans*? Today many Muslims are sure the answer is – neither. They believe that one should learn from other societies, but also from one's own, and try to take the best from them all: this is what their ancestors did long ago, and this is how they can best follow their religion and obey the teachings of the Prophet.

How to Find Out More

Unless you are a Muslim, you will not be allowed to go to Mecca. But all the countries of the North African coast, from Egypt to Morocco, are Islamic countries; so are Indonesia, Pakistan, Iran, and all the countries of the Arabian Peninsula. If you visit any of these lands, you will see the strength of Islam today, and the types of buildings described in this book.

There are mosques in Britain, such as the London Central Mosque in Regents Park and the one in Woking, in Surrey. If you visit a mosque, be careful to remove your shoes as you enter, as a sign of respect. But the best way to learn more about Islam is to ask a Muslim; there are many large cities in Britain which have a Muslim community.

You probably already know some of the legends of Arabian lands. If you wish to read them, try *Ali Baba*, *The Flying Horse*, or *Sinbad the Sailor* (Macdonald Educational).

These books should be available from libraries:

Shirley Kay, *The Arab World* (Oxford Children's Reference Library, Volume 13)
Riadh el-Droubie, *Islam* (Ward Lock)
Bernard Brett, *Mohammed* (Collins)
P.W. Crittenden, *Muhammad and Islam*
Islam in the Middle Ages
The Achievements of Islam (all Macmillan)
Duncan Townson, *Muslim Spain* (Cambridge University Press)
Robert Boyce, *The Story of Islam* (Religious Education Press)
John B. Taylor, *Thinking about Islam* (Lutterworth)
Muhammad Iqbal, *The Way of the Muslim* (Hulton)
Bernard Lewis, *The World of Islam* (Thames and Hudson)

Things to Do

1. Write a conversation between a Bedouin and a town-dweller in the time of Muhammad on the different ways they lived.
2. Draw a picture of a caravan travelling through the desert.
3. Look in your school or public library for modern stories of adventures in the desert.
4. Make a model of an Arab house (see page 62).
5. Read some of the Arabian Nights stories (e.g. 'Aladdin' or 'Ali Baba and the Forty Thieves'). You will probably find these in your school or public library.
6. Make your own map showing the lands where Islam is the chief religion today. Use an up-to-date atlas for this.
7. Find as many pictures as you can showing Muslim mosques and minarets, the way they decorate these, their books and other beautiful things. From these make your own book of Islamic art.
8. For class discussion:
   (a) The Muslim rules of 'Dos' and 'Don'ts': are they good rules? (See pages 24–27)
   (b) The Muslim idea of Dar al-Islam (peace for everyone inside Islam) and Dar al-Harb (war against everyone outside Islam): what do you think of this? (See pages 31–33)
   (c) The Muslim idea that God should be thanked for all food: do you agree? (See page 35)
9. Class project: Put on an exhibition for the school under the title The World of Islam. You could show maps, posters, postcards, your own drawings, models, samples of Arabic handwriting, costumes etc. You could also give short lectures (e.g. on the life of Muhammad, what Muslims believe, Islamic art and architecture) or write and act a play on the life of Muhammad.
10. If there is a mosque anywhere near you, try to visit it. If possible, get a Muslim to explain to you about their services and worship.

Time Chart

	Rule of the early Caliphs	*Baghdad and the East*	*North Africa*
AD 600	570 Birth of Muhammad 610 Muhammad starts preaching 622 The Hijra [1 AH] 632 Death of Muhammad RULE OF THE COMPANIONS 661 UMAYYAD RULE BEGINS	637 Muslims defeat Persian armies 642 Persian Empire ends	642 Fustat founded by Muslims
AD 700 [79 AH]	743 Umayyad Rule ends	750 ABBASID RULE BEGINS 762 Baghdad founded 786–809 al-Rashid	
AD 800 [179 AH]			868 Ibn Tulun become governor of Egypt
AD 900 [279 AH]			969 FATIMID RULE BEGINS from Egy Cairo founded al-Azhar mosque founded
AD 1000 [379 AH]		1055 Seljuks enter Baghdad	
AD 1100 [479 AH]			1169 Saladin takes Ca 1171 SALADIN BE-COMES SULTA 1193 Saladin dies
AD 1200 [579 AH]		1258. Last Abbasid ruler killed Mongols take Baghdad	1250 MAMLUK RU BEGINS 1260 Mamluk army defeats Mongols
AD 1300 [679 AH]			
AD 1400 [779 AH]			

Other Muslim events	*The outside world*	*Islamic men of learning*
635 Muslims take Damascus 636 Muslim forces defeat Byzantine armies 638 Muslims take Jerusalem 641 Muslims take Egypt		
711 Muslims begin conquest of Spain	732 Charles Martel turns back Muslims in France	
	800 Charlemagne becomes Holy Roman Emperor	Rhazes (physician) al-Buhturi (poet) al-Farabi (philosopher) al-Mutanabbi (poet)
1071 Seljuks defeat Byzantines	1066 Normans invade England 1097 First Crusade 1099 Crusaders capture Jerusalem	Ibn Sina (philosopher) al-Biruni (historian)
1187 Saladin takes Jerusalem	1147–8 Second Crusade 1189–92 Third Crusade	al-Idrisi (geographer) Ibn Rushd (philosopher)
1260 Mongols take Damascus	1204 Fourth Crusade 1215 Magna Carta 1261 End of Crusader rule in Constantinople	
		Ibn Battuta (traveller)

Glossary

Allah, Muslim name for God
alms, gifts given to the poor
apostle, someone sent from God to preach to people
architecture, the design of buildings
astrologer, someone who tries to discover from the stars what will happen to people
astronomer, someone who studies the movements of the stars
bazaar, Arab shopping centre
Bedouin, Arab people who wander in the desert
benefaction, money given for the purpose of helping other people
bountiful, giving many good things
brocade, silk with patterns woven in it
calamity, trouble
Caliph, title given to leaders who succeeded Muhammad: word means successor
calligraphy, art of writing beautifully
caravan, band of people travelling together across the desert
charity, giving to the poor
chest, box for storing things
cistern, tank for storing water
citadel, military headquarters
confectioner, sweet-maker
courtier, someone who attends a king or ruler in his court
covenant, solemn agreement
to create, to make
Creator, maker; here means God, creator of everything
crusade, here means the war of Christians against *Muslims*; word comes from cross-bearer
to declare, to speak
dorqaa, covered courtyard (Arabic)
dynasty, line of rulers succeeding each other
emigrant, someone who leaves his country to live somewhere else

falsehood, lie
fast, a time when, for the sake of religion, people eat and drink little or nothing
fragile, weak, easily broken
garlic, kind of onion with a strong smell
graven, written
hajj, Arabic word for the special journey to Mecca
han, Arabic word for travellers' lodging-house
hilt, handle of a sword
Imam, *Muslim* leader
inhabitant, someone who lives in a place
irrigation, network of channels carrying water over the fields
Islam, the religion started by Muhammad; the word means surrender to God
iwan, Arab word for the place of deepest shade in an Arab house
Kaba, most important place of worship in Mecca; word means cube
livelihood, way of earning a living
luxury, rich living
malkaf, shaft for drawing cool air down into an Arab house (Arabic)
manuscript, book written by hand
meteorite, stone which has fallen from the sky; the Meccans treasured one as a sacred stone
mihrab, place in a *mosque* wall which points towards Mecca (Arabic)
minbar, pulpit (Arabic)
minaret, tower from which the *muezzin* sang out the call to prayer
minority, group of people in some way different from most of the people round them
monk, man who belongs to a religious group in which he makes special promises and lives according to a special rule
mosque, *Muslim* place of worship
muezzin, *Muslim* leader who makes the call to prayer
mushrabeya, lattice window in Arab house to keep sun out and let air in (Arabic)
Muslim, someone who believes in the religion of *Islam*
to navigate, to steer towards the place you want to reach
navigator, someone who steers
oasis, fertile area round a well, spring or pool of water in the desert
papyrus, paper made from a kind of reed grown in Egypt
paradise, place of perfect happiness for good people after death
parchment, sheepskin scraped smooth and used for writing on
patriarch, head of the Byzantine Church
pharmacist, someone who makes medicines

pharmacology, *pharmacy*, science of making medicines
pilgrim, someone who makes a journey to a famous religious centre
pilgrimage, journey to a religious centre
porcelain, very fine china, much of it made in China
prophet, one who speaks the message of God to people
pyramid, famous Egyptian burial monument shaped like a triangle
qadi, Arab word for judge
quiver, case for holding arrows
Quran, sacred book of the *Muslims*, containing Muhammad's words from God
Ramadan, *Muslim* month of fasting
rite, ceremony
sahn, courtyard (Arabic)
salsabil, basin with water trickling through it (Arabic)
sanctuary, holy place
sanskrit, ancient language of India
scabbard, case to hold a sword
Sultan, *Muslim* ruler
surety, safety
suspended, hung
takshif, messenger who goes ahead of a caravan (Arabic)
teak, wood from a particular tree noted for its hardness
treachery, being disloyal to a ruler or leader
turban, scarf wound round the head to make a headdress
witness, someone who tells what he saw happening